RAINBOWS H.

RAINBOWS HAVE ECHOES

Julie Miller

ARTHUR H. STOCKWELL LTD
Torrs Park, Ilfracombe, Devon, EX34 8BA
Established 1898
www.ahstockwell.co.uk

ISBN 978-0-7223-4834-5
Printed in Great Britain by
Arthur H. Stockwell Ltd
Torrs Park   Ilfracombe
Devon EX34 8BA

DEDICATION

I dedicate my book to my husband, who enriched my
life beyond measure.
Terence Albert Miller, MBE, 1928–2014.
He taught me about endurance and I am so very grateful.

CONTENTS

FOREWORD BY LINDA ROBEY

Usually, when we are very close to something it is very hard to see its brilliance. To gain that objective distance, to fully observe, is not so easy when we are up close. And yet, the illumination and admiration I feel for my mother proves otherwise. These writings have allowed some space to reflect and gather together the pieces of what I see as my inheritance, my heritage and my inspiration.

The first third of this book recounts my mother's life from the age of twenty-two. It sets the scene of how her personality and character shape the way she coped with the devastating and destructive forces of dementia in my stepfather.

My mother knows the real meaning of value and demonstrates her gift to transform the broken. She sees the small things that can be overlooked and treasures moments like no other. She knows the meaning of celebration and is generous with her time, her thoughts and her love. She knows how to make people feel of worth. I have benefitted from this and so have my children. I am proud to be her daughter and hope that, through the story of her life and work, she will reach a wider audience and teach others how to cherish and mend.

When Mum gave up teaching, finally, I worried that she would lose her purpose and it would diminish her, but she is not made that way. Positively and bravely and with the flair of a magician she finds a new way to cherish life and those around her. Mum's unique creativity and wonder at the world is still vast and her ability to mend continues and grows in all of us.

Bless her, she is a blaze.

FOREWORD BY JULIE MILLER

Swinging, just swinging, in the children's play area at the George and Dragon pub in Apperley Bridge, Bradford, with my college friend Margaret Reed. We were an unlikely-looking pair of young girls – Margaret short and dark and me tall and blond – but our Yorkshireness held us together. Asian flu had hit Leicester University College of Education in 1957 and only two girls missed that ferocious illness – Margaret and I – and our reputation of strength, stamina and resistance grew; respect for the two Yorkshire lasses who took round tea and trays of nourishment to our fellow students for weeks on end grew almost beyond credibility.

As we la-la'd to the movement of our swings, Margaret said to me, "Why are you getting married next week?"

This remark took me completely by surprise and I fell silent, and even stopped la-la-ing for a moment or two.

Eventually I said to Margaret, "Don't know really. I think it might be that I worry no one else will ask me; and I'll be glad to leave home and run my own house and live as I like. That'll be really something."

Margaret's reply, in her delicious North Country accent: "But you are beautiful and clever."

INTRODUCTION

Two separate stories are in my head, separate but interdependent. The first is exciting, often alarming, frequently sad and bewildering and concerns two marriages – one lasting nearly ten years and ending in divorce and the other lasting over forty years and ending with dementia. This tale is alternatively entitled *There's a Wasp in the House* – the wasp being the irritant, hovering unseen and unpredictably ready to destroy peace of mind in seconds – buzzing noisily and causing the listener to be anxious and alert and watchful – the destroyer of peace of mind and harmony.

The story, which interweaves, is named *Rainbows Have Echoes* and follows my professional life of teaching English to students arriving in schools with no knowledge of the host language and frequently troubled by experiences of war and inhumane treatment.

This work has sustained me and empowered me even when my home-life circumstances were gut-wrenchingly disturbing. This work in schools, home and abroad, has been my lifeblood. The courage of the young people allotted to my care has taught me about bravery and made me even more determined to create a user-friendly and harmonious method of teaching English and to try and mend the world through my efforts to take a human being from a stressful place full of disquiet and pain to a sanctuary of peace where moments of joy can be shared in trust and security.

The raw courage of each new pupil facing me with fear in their eyes and in their demeanour inspires me in my efforts to create a programme for them which will hold their attention and give them hope for a sound educational future and more comfortable existence.

Rainbows Have Echoes is so called because placing respect, humour and love and a realistic ladder of learning into a child's life brightens and colours it and usually culminates in echoing memories into their future lives. My endeavour, in this book, is to blend the two aspects of wasp stings and rainbows into one coherent pattern or shape, which has been my experience so far. I am about to embark on the enterprise of my life.

CHAPTER 1

WASPS

I had met my husband-to-be at a dance at the Floral Hall in Bradford, now a mosque. He was an athletic man who resembled Richard Todd of the Robin Hood films. He had trodden on the back of my sandals and broken the strap by following me too closely up the stairs to the balcony. We had laughed together after I'd given him a bash with my handbag and then I'd danced the rest of the evening on my one bare foot with him. He was sporty, sexy, witty and obviously keen to be with me. He took me home in his old Ford Popular with a running board and instructions not to step on it.

I had also discovered he was really randy – so he met all my requirements for a suitable husband.

We were married the week after being questioned by my trusted friend in the George and Dragon pub garden, but not before I had inadvertently damaged his confidence in matters sexual. My wrong choice of words, I am certain, made him lose the confidence to believe in his own capacity to make love. Had I realised at the time that my choice of words would have such a profound impact on a sensitive and insecure man I might have explained myself immediately, but it is only on reflection that I can pinpoint the moment he lost his confidence.

CHAPTER 2

RAINBOWS

After leaving college, my first school was Barkarend Road Primary in the slum-clearance area of Bradford, West Yorkshire. In those days probationary teachers had to work for at least a year in the city which had provided them with a grant. In those days grants covered the cost of tuition, accommodation, food and transport. We were allotted schools and no preferences were taken into account, so I suspect they placed young newly qualified teachers in the most challenging areas. It was a kind of survival-of-the-fittest test, but I loved my school.

Many, many Sikh families were arriving from the Punjab and given temporary accommodation in homes about to be demolished. The indigenous children who already lived in the area were also disturbed by seeing neighbours' houses torn down by council demolition workers and suffered from the anxiety which that provoked.

This school's anxious inhabitants were very needy. They clung to what appeared to be stable. Each morning we would sell penny and halfpenny biscuits and again at break time. Most were dependent on free school meals, which arrived by van in huge metal containers.

One little girl, during a severe Yorkshire winter, arrived early wearing unsuitable clothes for the bleak northern weather.

The children were allowed to take shelter in the cloakroom and the outer door was opened by the caretaker at about eight o'clock. Along one wall were huge boiler pipes, which started to give off heat about the same time. This little girl, in an effort to obtain some warmth, cradled the pipe with her arms. At the start of the heating process, when the pipes were giving out a tiny amount of warmth, this small girl, called Shirley, waited for more warmth. By the time staff arrived Shirley was screaming. The pipe had expanded and trapped her arm between itself and the wall. I can still hear her screams. An ambulance was called. Firemen using crowbars prised the pipe away from the wall sufficiently to enable her arm to be released. Skin grafts were the order of the day, and she was many months in hospital because her skin had become fused with the pipes and remained there.

But the school was a good place, and it was there that my interest began in teaching English to non-English speakers – a passionate interest which remains to this day. The needier the child, the harder I worked to provide some respite from their harsh living conditions. I felt lucky to be there and the work was rewarding.

Each Saturday morning a contingent of my pupils arrived at my family home. My mum would give them juice and chocolate biscuits on a tray with a pristine white tray-cloth. Those children were impressed and thought us 'dead posh' even though we lived in a council house on a large estate. The children and I would walk down to the canal and we began to believe that life could be good.

CHAPTER 3

WASPS

The wrong choice of words in a sensitive situation can have disastrous consequences. Several months before our marriage we were in my future husband's home in Otley. His parents were out and he was making sexual advances, in which I was usually more than ready to play my part – but it was the wrong time of the month for me and I said, "No – you *can't*" instead of "No – you *mustn't*." Neil, my husband-to-be, must have taken it that I was doubting his capabilities and sexual prowess. From that moment on he became tentative and totally unsure of himself, and his sexual expectations and demands became so diminished they became almost non-existent. I became increasingly petulant. In fact, on our three-day honeymoon in London we stayed physically apart, with me taking long walks alone in the West End of London wearing my Russian-style fur hat and my long astrakhan honeymoon coat, feeling very low indeed and unattractive and totally undesirable. After the honeymoon, we returned to the cottage at Nab Wood near Keighley, a rented bungalow which we had kitted out with a lot of help from Neil's parents. We had the bare essentials for a lovely life with my continuing work in the slums of Bradford and Neil working as a physiotherapist at Pudsey Hospital.

With the physical side of our marriage almost zero, we would often stand at the bus stop waiting for the bus to take us into Bradford to work, without speaking. I believed myself now to be an unattractive married woman, so I brought a dog home for company and took to taking long walks along the canal banks a stone's throw from our first home. I threw myself into my schoolwork totally and wholeheartedly.

CHAPTER 4

RAINBOWS WITH SHARP EDGES

I gained a reputation for my energy and commitment, and for reaching the troubled children in my care and making them smile. The satisfaction I gained from my work made up somehow for my unsatisfactory and unhappy home life.

Because so many children in my class arrived with no knowledge of the English language I was at a loss to know where to begin. I realised that they absorbed spoken English relatively quickly, but was also quick to realise I had very few ideas regarding the teaching of literacy skills. The headmistress, Miss Stewart, told me to assess their levels of English (reading and writing) by administering two tests: the Burt Word Recognition Test and the Schonell Reading Test. These I duly administered and said, "But what do I do now?"

Her reply was "Administer the same tests in a few months' time and see if they have made progress."

These instructions seemed ludicrous to me. My common sense told me that this did not entail any actual teaching, so I said, "Those two tests both indicate that some words are actually easier to learn than others. There is an obvious incline of difficulty in those chosen words in the test."

Her reply was "Obviously."

I said, "If there is a sequence and a pattern to the English language, then I will find it and teach those words and their meanings methodically."

She replied, "Impossible!"

So began my journey, which took over my life for the next twenty-two years, logging every word hurdle, every mistake, on a grid system which filled notebook after notebook and totally absorbed me. Sometimes my spirit flagged, but never my interest and never believing for one thousandth of a second that the mission was impossible.

I moved words around, deleted some and highlighted others until I had a range of word lists with a common factor – in all 161 lists of words which ranged from basic, much used and familiar words to obscure, irregular and unfamiliar ones.

Using my lists I compiled my own 'book box scheme' so I had something for each child to read regardless of the strength of their English-language literacy skills.

I found that the children enjoyed the progression and appeared to hunger for the next pattern of words. This delighted me.

CHAPTER 5

MORE WASPS

Because my school holidays did not coincide with my husband's own hospital holidays, Neil's lack of interest in his work came to the surface. He would decide to stay at home if I was not at school and I would be asked to go to a neighbour's home (we had no phone) and ring the physio department and say he was too unwell to go to work. I objected more and more each time and the neighbour became suspicious of the calls. When I was asked, "Is your husband at home because you are on holiday?" I became really uneasy. So began my capacity to lie convincingly, and I decided to convince my husband to use his knowledge of the world of medicine in another field of work.

Physiotherapy was not his forte, nor his interest; nor had he any ambition to further his study or his skills. Physiotherapy was not his choice. Pushed into the closest training to medicine because his mother's drive for her son was for him to become a doctor like his best friend, Tom, he managed to survive the medical school in the field of physiotherapy. It was apparent to me that he was endeavouring to live his powerful mother's dream.

Had his parents bought him a garage and allowed his passion to mend any kind of machinery I think he would probably not have become the flawed personality he did become. I say to all parents allow your children their own dreams and aspirations. Encourage them to pursue their own interests with loving words and gestures.

Neil was interviewed for a job with British Drug Houses and managed to obtain work as a representative in the Lincolnshire area. We moved to Lincoln and bought a new Wimpey house on a huge housing estate at North Hykeham. For a short space of time life seemed more settled, and surprisingly we managed to produce two wonderfully perfect children: Linda, now fifty-two, artistic, articulate, pretty and compliant, and Christopher, now fifty-one, intelligent, observant, athletic and strong.

Because I was on maternity leave I was at home and dependent on Neil to keep his job going and pay the mortgage. He had a firm's car and a good salary dependent largely on orders for the new drugs he was promoting. Sadly and alarmingly, one month before my son was born, Neil was sacked from BDH. I knew it had been a likelihood because of Neil's impatient nature and his inability to perform the American-style 'hard sell'. On visiting doctors he would see a waiting room full of patients and leave samples of new products without actually seeing a doctor. It felt as if he was returning home before he even set off. He would often burn off petrol whilst the car was stationary in the driveway at home in order to convince any BDH inspector that he had been out on the road clocking up mileage on behalf of the drug firm and visiting doctors.

CHAPTER 6

A LITTLE RAINBOW

Before the arrival of my two children, and at the start of life in Lincoln, I was appointed to Mount Street Girls' School, whose catchment was mainly the daughters of RAF personnel at bases around Lincoln.

Again I could see the instability and insecurity which arises from the nomadic nature of moving from RAF base to RAF base. I became even more aware of the need to teach with a certainty. To adopt the demeanour of a well-prepared teacher who had planned out the detail of each lesson, which would then accommodate each and every pupil regardless of ability and make them feel not just valuable but also worthy of every scrap of my attention.

CHAPTER 7

WASPS TOGETHER WITH RAINBOWS

The feeling of hopelessness and helplessness wrapped itself round my being. I could not obtain work myself as my second baby was about to be born. Neil had no job and I couldn't teach.

The rep's car had to be returned. We had no money and all there was in my cupboard was a tin of Ajax and a tin of custard powder. We were without food, I had nothing to give my eighteen-month-old daughter and I was about to produce another child.

Neil decided to ride up to Yorkshire to borrow money from his parents. He had bought a second-hand motorbike on hire purchase, and he set off leaving me in a house we couldn't afford with a prenatal doctor's appointment at two o'clock that day.

I shook the crumbs left in my empty biscuit tin into Linda's hand and she ate them, and just as we were about to set off for the doctor's appointment there was a knock on the door. Two men stood there demanding money due on the motorbike. I told them I had no money to pay the due instalments, so they said that they had to take the bike as no money had been paid since the deposit. As Neil was away on the bike I had to send them away. I think they felt quite sorry for me, and said they would return another day when my husband was at home.

I took my tear-stained face to the doctor's, where my blood pressure was pronounced high. I knew it would be hours before Neil got home. By then shops were shut for the day and we were very hungry – and this is when a rainbow slipped into a wasps' nest and reshaped the world.

Pushing my pushchair home, feeling achingly sad and lonely, I trudged back to my Wimpey house. Then God smiled.

A window opened and a friend shouted out, "I've been knocking on your door to invite you to Vanessa's birthday party. Come now – it's started."

Linda and my big-tummied self went in to see many children and a table groaning with party food. Tiny sandwiches with the crusts cut off, sausage rolls, sausages with cheese, jellies, fairy cakes and an enormous birthday cake were in front of us. We must have appeared like Dickensian waifs and strays. We could not contain our hunger or our delight and tucked in with enthusiasm. Our rainbow had arrived.

Two weeks later my son was born. My waters had broken long before his birth and I struggled to cope with what is known as a dry birth, but he was here and safe and I loved him with every atom of my being.

Because of the difficult birth he was rather jaundiced and his baby skin had been unprotected. Rashes appeared all over his tiny body, even in his ears and on his eyelids, which made him very restless and he cried a lot and slept little.

At night I would rest his carrycot across the well of my dressing table and sit on my bed watching him struggle to breathe, his head twitching from side to side as if searching for oxygen.

I said in my head, "Please, God, if You let him live I will never ever complain about anything again."

Linda slept and Neil snored, but my vigil went on and on. What were we to do? I feared my children would be taken from me because we were unable to care for them.

Neil heard of a private physiotherapy practice in Barrow-in-Furness which was for sale. After much negotiation with Abbey National and Barclays Bank we managed to obtain a mortgage and bought the practice – a huge end-of-terrace Victorian building with two physiotherapy surgeries and a chiropody room and plenty of living space, and it was right next to the large park complete with duck ponds, a bandstand and play areas for children. But no one could have been more unsuited to running a business than my husband. The wasps were certainly buzzing.

He would decide that he was now an entrepreneur with no limits to his abilities. He would practise as a chiropodist without qualifications and perform electrolysis on trusting women with facial hair. Even after failing the exam to become registered, he continued to expand his failing enterprise. He rented a room behind a hairdressing salon in Grange-over-Sands and I would travel each weekend to clean it and make it presentable. I would go on the train from Barrow with my two small children and hope they would play happily in the adjoining courtyard whilst I cleaned up the most appalling messes: toenail clippings, swabs, trailing unwound electric cables, eggshells, old toast and mouldy cups of cold tea and coffee. I would then return to Barrow with Neil driving his second-hand Jaguar car – another misjudged status symbol. The business was struggling. He believed that it was fine to spend the money if he was paid in cash and bank any cheques. This wasn't working, and our accountant became increasingly concerned.

In an effort to help our financial situation I pushed my pram containing my toddler, Christopher, with Linda sitting neatly on the end between the handles, to the education offices. Of course, if I let go of the handle the pram would tip and send my babies flying.

I had no appointment, but I marched in, demanding to talk to anyone responsible for teaching jobs.

CHAPTER 8

A RAINBOW PEEPS IN

At that time in Barrow-in-Furness female teachers who were married were not given permanent contracts. The nearest place for any permanence was to take up employment in Lancashire, so I took up the temporary job offered in a junior school one and a half miles from my home. I employed a nanny for Linda and Christopher, which left me free to cycle twice a day to school – twice because I would go home at lunchtime believing no one was really equipped to feed my two little children. Christopher climbed everything and I needed to check on his safety.

I was given a class of thirty seven-year-olds, the equivalent of Year 3 in present-day terms. Amongst this class of children was a boy who always sat in the same place and often appeared to fall asleep. Around his chair the parquet floor was discoloured and rotten. I very soon discovered that the discolouration was due to the fact that he frequently wet himself, and the floor had to be mopped with disinfectant each time, so sadly he was always made to sit in the same place.

Smart-arse that I was in those days, I thought I had the problem sussed by reminding him to visit the toilet every twenty minutes. But this did not sort out the difficulty, so I just kept a mop and bucket handy and tried very hard not to indicate in any way that I thought he was freaky. I gave it my best shot to include him in every aspect of my teaching time with him and grew very fond and extremely protective towards this small sweet-faced boy.

The time came for my infants to be introduced to the junior school across the playground. A senior teacher with a close affinity to Hitler lined up my class in the corridor and suddenly broke the silence by screaming abuse at my boy. He had weed on the floor. Spitting abhorrence and vengeance, she told him that babies could not go to junior school.

I said, very fiercely, "Don't treat him like that. He would never do it on purpose."

There was stunned silence and I grabbed my boy and propelled him swiftly to the cupboard where we kept clean trousers, socks and underpants.

The headmistress called me to her office. She was an elderly spinster and I knew she was fair, but she was very angry.

"You can't talk to a member of staff like that. I cannot have you on my staff. Remember you are temporary."

My response was "No child would ever wee himself on purpose. There must be something wrong. He must get some advice from the medical profession. He is suffering a lot."

The following week I was called into the head's office once again. She said, "If I could appoint you on to my permanent staff I would. Your boy has petit mal. There is a more permanent job for you on Walney Island if you want it. It is a special school, with pupils who would benefit from your heart-warming care and your bravery."

And so I moved to Richard Brunskill School on Walney Island. One year spent in this wonderful school consolidated every idea I had ever had in finding a way of teaching which would nurture feelings of success and joy in young people who were struggling to find a pathway to learning and a safe foothold in their educational pursuits.

CHAPTER 9

WASPS WITH THE HOPE OF A RAINBOW

Anyone who knew my husband's character would have predicted that the business would fail, and it did. He was lazy, dishonest and utterly self-indulgent.

Neil came up with the idea of emigrating to a new country. This struck me as a sound-enough venture. I thought that to have oceans between my little family and my controlling mother-in-law might help to heal our marriage, which was at breaking point.

We decided that New Zealand was the likeliest-sounding destination and we made enquiries. The principal, who was also head of the physiotherapy school at the teaching hospital, wrote to us desperate for qualified physiotherapists – we would receive paid passage for the four of us – and we jumped at the opportunity.

We couldn't sell the practice, but we managed to sell the property as a home. Selling the equipment was fraught with difficulties, but we managed eventually to sell plinths and machinery to a health spa in Ilkley. After a prolonged seaman's strike we set sail from Tilbury Docks on 16 December 1966.

CHAPTER 10

A WONDERFUL RAINBOW

Curaçao, Panama, Tahiti – what a cruise! Wonderful, exciting and a real adventure. In Tahiti I was singled out – unbelievably singled out – as a beautiful English girl. Wow! I was now twenty-eight years old and had been convinced by my husband that I was unattractive, not just to him but to anyone who might have given me a second look.

Our ship, the *Rangitane*, had anchored off Tahiti and we were welcomed by singing flower-throwing natives in colourful canoes. We decided to use the babysitting service on board ship to go to a highly recommended Tahitian nightclub.

Through the Bay of Biscay I had suffered a very bad bout of seasickness. I was doing my utmost to care for my children. Linda would have her fifth birthday on the day we crossed the equator, and Christopher was a very active and adventurous three-and-a-half-year-old. I was really struggling to be alert and watchful and also keep up with my bouts of vomiting.

An elderly man said, "You look so ill – where is your husband? I have been a ship's captain and I know about seasickness."

I replied, "I think he's playing deck tennis or deck quoits."

He said, "You shouldn't be here looking after little ones. You should be lying down in your cabin," and he went off, only to come back five minutes later with a glass of brandy and three dry ship's biscuits.

Gradually I began to feel better, and by the time we reached Tahiti I was slimmer and quite sun-kissed. My self-confidence was returning, and as I walked through the avenue of palm trees smelling the hibiscus and listening to the beautiful sound of buzzing cicadas I felt good about myself for the first time in many, many years.

At the open-air nightclub we watched the traditional Tahitian dancers as they performed to the spellbinding and infectious drumming. It was then that the professional dancers split up from their group and each one moved amongst the audience and chose a new partner. I was amongst the chosen few, selected by a bronze and handsome French-speaking Tahitian male. I danced – the rhythms pulsating through me like an intoxicating lifeblood.

As he escorted me back, I said, *"Merci"* and he said, *"Vous êtes très, très belle."*

What a wonderful moment for me! I felt so alive and enormously happy and privileged to be in amongst such life-affirming joyful people.

We sailed on and arrived in Wellington on their hottest day for eleven years. I thought I was in the tropics. We had been booked on the Cook Strait ferry, which would transport us from North Island to South Island, from Wellington to Lyttelton. It was an overnight crossing and I was seasick again. We had two sets of bunk beds to enable us to sleep during the night-time crossing. Linda was completely disorientated. She had sampled and enjoyed dry land in Wellington and now the sea was heaving us about again as we crossed the notoriously turbulent water between the two islands of New Zealand known as the Cook Strait.

As I struggled to rest Linda suddenly sat bolt upright, climbed down the wooden ladder from the top bunk and weed on the rug between the sets of bunk beds, then climbed back up the ladder and snuggled back to sleep. In the dim light I could see a large wet patch on the rug. Desperate not to be challenged by any ship's stewards who would bring in early tea, I descended my own ladder, picked up the weed-on rug and exchanged it for the dry one in the cabin opposite – which was, fortunately, empty of passengers.

Once disembarked, we had then to travel by train to Dunedin, where we had been promised accommodation for the four of us. We were graciously welcomed at Dunedin Railway Station after travelling on the narrow-gauge, wooden-seated rickety train for hours on end. We had travelled almost the entire length of South Island, stopping at various stations for us to rush off the train for refreshments – no services on those trains. They sold Weet-bix (Weetabix here in the UK), toast and jam and hot and cold drinks. Christopher had knocked his head on the edge of a wooden-slatted seat, so we looked a tired-and-bedraggled foursome. The greetings were so warm and welcoming and so very helpful. We were driven by car to our new temporary home. The occupants were away on holiday for two weeks, so we had just a fortnight to find ourselves more-permanent rented accommodation.

The house was a rather neglected home belonging to a single mum with two children. She worked in the physio department of the hospital, but the bed linen was clean and I was delighted to find a huge array of Dr Seuss books which were new to me. Both my children enjoyed *Yertle the Turtle* and *Horton Hears a Who* almost as much as I enjoyed reading them out loud to them. Because we had adjusted the clocks hour by hour to each new time zone as we crossed the vast oceans we were not affected by disorientation, tiredness or jetlag, as many are if they travel long distances by plane.

During that fortnight whilst Neil familiarised himself with his hospital work, I shopped, cooked, played with the children and looked for a new and more-permanent home to rent, and together we bought an old van.

Many things surprised me: the shanty-town appearance of the red tin roofs of the hundreds of bungalows rising up from Otago Harbour in the surrounding hillsides; Chinese gooseberries, now renamed in the UK as kiwi fruits; pavlovas; fillet steaks; oysters and chips; the freshness of the air; and the friendliness of the Maori people. Surprisingly (to me) there seemed no tension or division between the indigenous people and the Pakehas – us (new settlers). This harmony continued to please me throughout my stay in this beautiful country.

A few days after our arrival in Dunedin, whilst parking our new 'old' van – new-looking because there is no pollution to cause the rust which corrodes metal in the more industrialised parts of the world – we spotted a familiar face. How could that be? We were as far away from our English home as it was possible to get. It was Pauline and Charles Higham and their beautiful baby boy, Tom. Familiar to us because they had been passengers on our ship, the *Rangitane*, travelling with us to New Zealand. They had brought their own car from the UK, but it was still being processed in Wellington and wouldn't arrive for some days.

I had spotted this young couple on board and had looked at Pauline with envy. She was everything I wasn't: she was poised, elegant and carried her chubby infant around the ship with enormous dignity, always calm, always sweet-faced. After we had greeted each other they climbed into the back of our van. We folded the pushchair and went to our rented house for a cup of tea. So much to talk about, so much to pass on to each other regarding our first few days in Dunedin.

Pauline had cried throughout the first few days in Dunedin. Charles was concerned because his wife was so homesick. He believed she would never settle. Charles had been appointed as a senior lecturer in anthropology at Otago University. He was an Oxford graduate, a rugby player and hugely ambitious. He was unnervingly academic and talented, and as the years went by our friendship grew and our lives became intertwined forever.

Pauline and Charles's family grew into four children – Tom, James, Emma and Caroline – and we shared so much in New Zealand. We are the greatest of friends to this day.

Charles's career in social anthropology soared to the dizzy heights of him obtaining the chair of the anthropology department. He was, at the age of thirty, the professor of anthropology at the university.

Neil's career spiralled downwards and we were, again, taking backward steps in my desperate bid to live a good life.

CHAPTER 11

WASPS – DEFINITELY A STING

Way back before we left the UK, when we were still in Barrow-in-Furness, but well on the way to fulfilling our plan to emigrate to New Zealand, Neil had to organise passports and visas. In those far-off days children did not need individual passports; they could be placed on their parents' documents.

Neil came home from his 'sorting out of official papers' day and handed me my own passport, which had its corner clipped and was thus unusable and had been negated. Neil was now the sole passport holder with me and the children as his dependants. I felt sick and utterly violated. I did not then realise what an awesome and terrible violation this actually was. I was no longer my own person; but even then I hadn't realised the depth of the dangers which could materialise as well as the anxieties which would emerge as we ventured into volatile and often hostile areas of the world, where without a passport one could quickly be put in danger. To own a British passport was, without question, an invaluable asset and one worthy of safekeeping. I had to keep one eye not only on my passport-holding husband, but also on my very adventurous, inquisitive son, who would dart off the second we let go of his hand, which he was usually reluctant to hold.

Anyone might believe that our lives were now sublime. We had obtained a rented bungalow at Andersons Bay, a wonderful spot overlooking the bays of St Clair and St Kilda. Our new home had a wilderness of a garden, but delightful verandas on three sides, three bedrooms, a lounge, a dining room and a kitchen.

We had just been pipped at the post to gaining a cosy bungalow nearer the town centre by our new-found Pommie friends. I will never forget the outside toilet there, down a few stone steps with instructions on the door which read, 'Do not switch on light – or be blasted from Grot.' Pauline and Charles had obtained this rented bungalow just an hour before we searched it out.

But we had transport to take Christopher to nursery; and Linda had begun school at Maori Hill Junior School, where my charming, quiet and pretty daughter was quickly making friends.

I had been appointed as teacher in the primary department of a boys' boarding school. Perfect, anyone would believe, but my husband was rapidly making enemies. Now a new group of people were discovering my husband's frailties. He was careless, lazy, greedy, unscrupulous and also totally dishonest. I seemed to spend my time apologising and making excuses for his many mistakes. He decided that he should train to be a teacher of physiotherapy. Surprisingly he was accepted on the course, but, because his study times were optional and self-regulated, his willpower failed him and all could see why he was failing the examinations, which came in three-monthly sections. My husband was asked to resit a paper which would be a deciding factor in the further pursuit of the diploma.

Neil said, "I'm going to study all day. Take the children off – don't let them bother me. I need to concentrate undisturbed all today."

Off the three of us went in my little car full of buckets, spades, sun hats, footballs, swimming togs and towels. I think it was the day of the worst thunderstorm in history. We ate Hokey-pokey ice cream sitting in wet clothes in a shelter at St Kilda and fish and chips in a shelter at St Clair then knocked on the door of a friend, but she had visitors – family members of her German husband who had recently arrived from Germany. We made a quick exit, and I drove around until seven o'clock with my children sitting miserably in the back of the car moaning.

Arriving back, I found my husband drinking tea surrounded by sawdust. He had adapted an easy chair by building a bookrest on to it to hold his textbooks with a piece which spun around to create a writing block. It even had a pen holder. Ingenious, but infuriating because he hadn't actually done any studying at all.

He waited for me to praise his efforts, but I couldn't. I was swallowing my annoyance with great difficulty.

CHAPTER 12

A RAINBOW FOR ME

Amongst the staff of my boys' boarding school was a science teacher who intrigued me more than any other member of staff. He had written books on survival, obtained his wings as a New Zealand Air Force pilot and was enormously confident, self-assured and charismatic. He was popular with the students and helpful with my young pupils.

Most coffee breaks we would sit together chatting and familiarising each other with our own histories. His shoulder would often be pressed close to mine, and this felt exciting and rather naughty. Quite often I would find a rose on the desk in my classroom.

I was sure it was from him, so one day I plucked up a little courage and said, "Are the roses from your garden?"

He replied, "Obviously. Have you loads of other admirers?"

Wow!

One day I found a bird with a broken wing. I placed it in a cardboard box and told my new friend about it. My little family had by now moved from Andersons Bay after being offered a school house on the campus, so home was very near work for me.

He made up some plaster of Paris and arrived with

mending materials to fix the bird at my kitchen table. I watched him tenderly fixing the bird's wing and I was shaking, not for the bird's welfare but with a kind of exhilarating lust.

He stood up and stretched out his arms and put them around me, saying, "We'll find somewhere quiet to be together one day – if that's all right with you."

It certainly was OK with me. My life had taken a very interesting and exciting turn.

CHAPTER 13

WASPS AGAIN

Christmas in New Zealand is, of course, in high summer. School holidays were long and most people had holiday homes called cribs. Many of them were near Queenstown, Naseby or Arrowtown and usually by lakes or overlooking the sea.

Hospital workers and medical staff did not, of course, have the same long holidays as schools. This did not suit my husband. He wanted to be at home if I wasn't working. He wanted to potter or play golf on the adjacent course just off Balmacewen Road, where our home was on the slopes of Flagstaff. It was my school holiday, but Neil set off with his golf clubs, instructing me to say he was too unwell to go to work. I rang the hospital.

At lunchtime, the principal of the teaching hospital, and Philip, the vice principal, arrived to enquire as to the well-being of Neil. As I was stumbling and fumbling to find words of explanation, in walked Neil with his golf clubs over his shoulder and he was whistling. That was the end of any respect he might have earned from senior colleagues.

CHAPTER 14

A BIT OF A RAINBOW

Although it might appear that I am totally dismissive and critical of my first husband, there were many times when I felt very loving and protective towards him, and often the excuses I made for his behaviour contained my own responsibility for his conduct. I was too needy, too demanding, not careful enough with money or too certain I was in the right. For my two beautiful children I was grateful. Sometimes I could detect an element of pride as he introduced me to someone new. He was inspired mechanically and would spend hours inside his own and other people's car engines. He always got broken vehicles running sweetly again and he had a brilliant sense of humour. He was often invited to parties for his endless capacity to entertain and could remember and tell jokes until listeners collapsed with laughter.

Neil was in the wrong field of work. We should not allow our parents to use us to make their dreams come true. The repercussions are too extensive and too life-limiting.

Now our lives in New Zealand became unstable and eventually untenable. Neil felt under threat and was constantly rebuked by senior staff at the teaching hospital. He talked of applying for work in other parts of the world once he had obtained his teaching diploma in physiotherapy. He failed exam after exam, with each failure making a further dent in his confidence and self-esteem. However, he never blamed himself. It was always another person's malicious intent to bring him down. It was agony for me because he was pressing his own self-destruct button. It was also agonisingly sad because I was so happy in my schoolwork and I had my new-found interest in another man.

CHAPTER 15

AM I ALLOWED TO CALL THIS A RAINBOW?

Each school morning the whole staff, both primary and secondary teachers, would assemble in the vast dining room of this large college for boys, where tea and coffee would be served along with savoury snacks and home-made biscuits. We would pull out the long wooden benches, leaving a space between the benches and the dining table.

On one magical summer's day, as I sipped my coffee, the new interest in my life squeezed along the bench behind me and I felt a real pressure in the small of my back. Then came the electrifying realisation that the pressure was his erect penis digging into my body through layers of clothing from behind. He moved to the end of the bench, turned and then faced me.

He looked straight into my eyes and said, "That's what you do to me."

Never in my life had I had such a thrilling and exhilarating moment as this. I was not simply a woman – I was a new woman. The world felt different and I was alive and desirable. I could not let go of this new existence and I would never be the old Julie again.

We did find some secret places to be on our own. This new man was attentive, passionate about his interest in me, aware, confident, intelligent and spiritually alert.

In fact, everything I felt I had missed from a partner. But, sadly for me, he was married. Whatever reasons I came up with to cold-shoulder him, I had a million other reasons to want to be near him.

We did find a very secret corner which felt so safe and concealed, and there I discovered a beautiful oasis to really be with this exciting man. There he made love to me – gently, confidently and lovingly. I was discovering a new life which I hadn't known existed. Delight and awe reached me, and I felt enriched rather than guilt-ridden.

Everything around me felt new and bright and exciting. I was no longer an unattractive woman and the world was electrifying and interesting. I wondered, 'Does behaving irresponsibly set you free?'

CHAPTER 16

A WASP STING BECOMES INFECTED

Neil realised he must leave the hospital. He was, reluctantly, awarded the teaching certificate provided he left Otago Teaching Hospital. That is what I was told, but I dared not question the validity of this with the hospital authorities.

Neil applied to Winnipeg, Vancouver, Tokyo and Hong Kong. Each of these hospital boards sent him offers of work in their main teaching hospitals, but within weeks letters arrived stating an apology and informing him that the post was already filled and they had withdrawn their offer. It must have been his references. In those days the transmission of information was by post, telephone or, in some cases, telegram.

At the dead of night, unknown to me, Neil used his master key to gain access to the physio department, broke into the principal's private office and somehow gained access to the confidential filing cabinet containing copies of private documents, including his own references. He copied the devastating information, closed the cabinet and returned home.

It was stated that Neil was 'the most spiritually and morally impoverished human being' the principal had ever had the misfortune to meet. He would never obtain work with those credentials.

Neil decided that the best plan was to return home to the UK, so I informed the bursar at my school of our intention.

He said, "Stay – let your husband go back to England. You stay in your own school house with your children. We value your work. Please stay."

Did he know more than I had told him about my circumstances?

But . . .

CHAPTER 17

DOUBLE JEOPARDY

. . . I had no passport of my own. Neil held the passport; the children and I belonged to him. I was told that a passport in my own right could only be obtained in my country of origin. I had to leave all I had grown to love and return to the UK. I would stay in the UK for a year, be with my parents and brother and return to New Zealand complete with a new passport and my children, to a complete and fulfilling life.

That was my plan.

The fourth and final year of our time in New Zealand was taken up with plans for our journey home. I needed to teach, I needed my children; but whilst my escapes with 'my new man' were exciting, they were not absolutely essential to my well-being, and he had a wife and a home and was respected in his work. I loved my time with him, but I was not in love. I could manage without wrecking too many lives. But he had managed to make me feel like a desirable woman. I would come back in a year's time and see what would then transpire.

As a family we had enjoyed wonderful holidays. Danseys Pass, Queenstown, Naseby and Arrowtown. We had visited North Island and Rotorua, experiencing the Glowworm Caves and being taken to underground hot-geyser water baths. Sublime experiences. I had also been eaten alive by sandflies whilst driving through the lush vegetation of the West Coast. We had shut the children in the car whilst we stood spraying fly killer in the air as Neil battled to mend a puncture.

We had holidayed in Nelson. We set off to visit a recommended beach called Kaiteriteri, several miles from Nelson. We got back to Nelson about five in the evening. The beach at Nelson was deserted. I thought everyone had gone home for tea. I stripped off and swam out in order to cool off before we went back to the bed and breakfast for our evening meal. The children sat on the beach with Neil, eating ice creams whilst I enjoyed my swim. As we got back to our tiny hotel the landlady's eyebrows shot upwards.

She said, "Your hair is wet – have you been swimming?"

I told her I had and that it was glorious and the water was heavenly and I had the beach to myself.

She replied with the horrifying words, "Didn't you hear the shark warning?"

The lifeguards had cleared the beach and then gone home. I was so very lucky as I had swum far out that day.

During that last year I had lived through two more experiences which changed the way I managed my life.

The way I taught the children entrusted to my care had changed since I had children of my own. I had grown to realise that other mothers were as fiercely protective of their offspring as I was of mine. This might sound rather a trite and overused expression; but before I had experienced motherhood, teaching was a kind of power game where I was able to use my powers of storytelling and drama to simply catch the attention of my pupils. Teaching in a private school was also a learning time for me. If you didn't please the parents, you didn't please the school.

On the final day of term time, before each holiday, we would have a tiny party. In the summer we would have juice and chocolate biscuits and in the winter we would have hot chocolate and cakes.

My class consisted of nineteen boys. There were one or two boarders and the rest were day boys. I adored each and every one of them and especially Matthew. I had taught his older brother, and his family were solidly and totally good people. The two brothers were intelligent and cooperative, but Matthew was particularly appealing because of his cheeky dimpled smile and his wonderful sense of fun and adventure. This particular end-of-term party, precious because it was my final year in my adopted country, Matthew was unusually active. He was stepping off and on his chair repeatedly and we all thought it was one of his jokes, so we all joined in the merriment and laughter.

Later that evening I had a phone call. A high-pitched distressed voice said, "What have you done to Matthew? Have you poisoned him? He is in hospital unconscious." It was Matthew's mother ringing from the hospital.

I just kept saying, "Oh no! Oh no! I haven't done anything to Matthew. I will ring around and ask if anyone else is ill."

I knew most boys would have gone back to their remote sheep farms or to their cribs or to the even more remote Gilbert and Ellice Islands. I managed to reach the assistant bursar, and he said he would contact the rest. I was sick with stress and worry and struggled to dial numbers with trembling hands and blurred vision. Every person we managed to reach said they were well and safe. I couldn't sleep and sat by the phone all night praying that no one would ring and say they were ill.

At six thirty in the morning the phone rang. It was Matthew's mother.

Matthew never regained consciousness. He died in the night and there was nothing we could have done. I am told it was a brain aneurysm. I am also told it could have happened at any time.

The phone went dead and this beautiful mother had lost her beloved young son. However do you pick up the pieces of your life trying to come to terms with such a loss? Perhaps I should have curtailed his excitable movements. Perhaps I should not have given him hot chocolate. Perhaps I should have been more vigilant. Perhaps I shouldn't have had parties at the end of term. Perhaps I was just a silly ill-informed teacher.

Matthew's mother came to see me just after the funeral. I kept my Christopher out of the way in case it was too painful for her to see me with my own small son, but she put her arms around me and said, "Sorry. Matthew loved you. Thank you for making him happy in his short, short life."

We cried desperate tears together and I gave her a loose-leaf booklet with messages from all his classmates and from me.

CHAPTER 18

RAINBOWS APPEAR

My boarding school was to be inspected by the New Zealand Inspectorate. I was very nervous and apprehensive and agitated. My marriage was in fragments, and to add to the moral and spiritual disintegration of my husband he would play squash for hours in the new squash court and return home without showering. He always wore nylon shirts and shorts and he would eat huge quantities of food very quickly, belching and farting and patting his huge belly. He resembled Friar Tuck, but without the joviality.

Had I caused this decline in my partner? Was I to blame? Perhaps his flawed personality could not cope with the wrong choice of work. To add to my self-doubt was the fact that a precious child had died on my watch.

In my favour, although it was almost in my subconscious mind, I was a much better teacher after I had children than before. This notion was reflected in how I performed in the classroom. The loss of Matthew had deeply affected me and I knew I had to be more alert, more certain, and ensure that each of my pupils would believe that the next piece of learning would be even more exciting than the last. It would be just within reach and just around the corner. This became my mantra. We studied life in Mexico and made piñatas. We studied Japan and cooked Japanese food and used chopsticks. We climbed Flagstaff hill and organised lifts to the anthropology department of Otago University to study the most recent archaeological findings from Thailand.

The inspection happened.

My inspector said, "This teacher would be an outstanding asset to any educational establishment. She has taken my breath away and she has her boys hungry for the next piece of learning. I am in awe of the way she conducts her lessons."

This was indeed a rainbow moment.

This was my life as a teacher.

I could make a difference.

It was recognised that I had something of value to offer the world. My spirits were lifted. I could set my targets high. I wanted to be and needed to be brilliant in my professional field. Even if my relationship with Neil was in pieces I was proud of my athletic, friendly and popular son and my beautiful daughter, who was so eager to please and who shadowed me. We shared the same delight in living things and sunsets and sunrises. She was awestruck at the sighting of a dragonfly and would gaze in wonderment. There was a stillness in her appreciation of the marvels which nature provided.

One neighbour had disconcertingly shaken me by saying, "You'll never be dead while she's alive."

CHAPTER 19

WASPS REAPPEAR

The clocks ticked on to the moment we were to leave New Zealand. We were not to travel by train this time. We were to fly from Mamona Airport to Wellington, where our *Northern Star* vessel was to take us home to Tilbury.

But not before my husband had very nearly cocked up our planned eight-week voyage.

We had paid the deposit for a four-berth cabin on B deck. Our ship, the *Northern Star*, was to take the long eight-week cruise to England, stopping off at Rarotonga, Tahiti, Acapulco, Panama, Trinidad, Barbados and Lisbon.

I went to see the travel agent to complete the payment. It was much less than I expected. The agent saw my shocked reaction and asked me what was amiss. I told him it was half what I expected to pay.

He said, "Oh, but your husband phoned a month ago and said you were getting off at Acapulco, hiring a car and travelling overland through the Americas with your two little children and I had to rearrange your passage."

I burst into tears. The travel agent disappeared and his assistant said he was unwell and being sick in the back of the shop!

I tearfully stated, "Oh, so anyone can ring up and cancel someone else's booking!"

Neil and I, later in the day, went back to the agent to sort it. His assistant said that the agent had gone home ill, but they had rebooked our continuing passage to Tilbury; however, we now had to change cabins at Acapulco and move to another on C deck.

I said, "Over my dead body will we move."

Neil said, "She means it."

He thought the whole adventure would be a nice surprise for me. A big mistake!

So we said our farewells at Mamona Airport, anxious about how secure our cabin would be once on board. We had sold our furniture; our heavy trunk, with the rest of our belongings, had arrived in Wellington. We were off, but not before a question was asked me by a mother of one of my pupils just before I left the airport.

"My son keeps asking me what you mean by *bish*."

"*Bish*", I said, "is not a word I use. When do I say that?"

"When you have them out on the playing field. He asks you if he can go back into school to use the toilet and you say, 'Bisharp.'"

"Oh," says me, recognising a Yorkshire colloquialism, "I mean 'Be sharp' like in 'Be quick.'" Language sorted!

CHAPTER 20

RAINBOWS AND WASPS

We sailed from Wellington to Auckland overnight, so we were still in New Zealand. I rang 'my man'. He cried and said he had sat in my vacated house and felt desolate. I had left a leather cigarette box near the kettle and he would send it by post to my parents' address in Bradford. The leather box had been a gift from him, so I felt like a betrayer having left it behind.

Several days into our long cruise home Linda had become unusually fretful. She was normally the most uncomplaining child I had ever met. There was to be a fancy-dress parade on the main deck. All I had was some orange and green crêpe paper, so I painstakingly dressed her up as a carrot. She couldn't move her arms without tearing the paper and she had green paper leaves sprouting from the top of her head. She felt hot, but the weather was tropical so I let her queue up to be judged with all the other dressed-up characters.

That dear, brave, long-suffering and precious daughter of mine had mumps. As I removed the crêpe paper her neck was swollen level with her chin.

The ship's doctor refused to deal with her because he had never had mumps himself and was fearful of infection. I was told by the nurse that mumps can be a really agonising, dreadful and destructive illness in males.

Linda was put in isolation and from that wing of the ship we could look down on the deck where Neil was the anchorman in the tug of war – passengers versus crew. A loathing and bitterness crept into my being. I'd had to put Christopher in the nursery because I couldn't depend on my husband to keep him safe.

Linda got well again as we sailed on to Tahiti, where to my absolute delight I was chosen to dance again. I was feeling quite positive about our future. One amusing episode in Tahiti happened as we walked from the nightclub back to the *Northern Star*. Halfway back to the ship, with the Pacific Ocean glittering to our left, we came across a refreshment hut with flaps both sides, so one could see customers waiting to be served from one side of the hut to the other. Although I was a mother and very nearly thirty-two years old, I was quite unworldly and rather naïve.

An attractive raven-haired woman was gazing at me from the opposite side of the refreshment hut. She was staring, then said, "You like-a the cock? Me no like-a the cock."

To the amusement of our friends who had visited the nightclub with us, I replied, "Yes, thank you very much. It's nice."

They then told me I was being propositioned by a lesbian. Crikey! I must be full of allure. I was teased about it for the rest of the journey.

Across the vast oceans we travelled and arrived at Acapulco in Mexico. The ship's purser had told me to carefully watch my two blond-haired children as youngsters looking like my two were often kidnapped and sold into slavery. We didn't take them more than

100 yards from the safety of the ship, but at night we arranged for babysitters on board to care for our two precious children once they were safely in our cabins and asleep.

We had heard of the nightclub where you could watch the divers. Young men would stand on a clifftop overlooking a beautiful bay. They would have to judge to the millisecond when to dive into the narrow inlet. This was where the tide freakishly changes the depth of water from a few feet to about thirty feet. Many had died misjudging their timing and we were intrigued. The nightclub was splendid. Tiers and tiers of levels so all visitors had views of these spectacular feats. There was a Mexican band and a tiny dance floor and wonderful food being served to many of the people watching.

We decided to order some food. No one else in our party had pesetas or even American dollars, which would have been acceptable. So in my innocence – or ignorance – I had said, I have loads of traveller's cheques. I will pay."

When it was time to pay, the waiter handed me the bill and I handed him a traveller's cheque for the sum of $50. The waiter shook his head and went off only to return with the manager, who held out his hand and called for pesetas. He then went off only to return with an armed policeman.

At this point I was more afraid than I had ever been in my life, with the realisation that I had no documents, no passport and a husband I didn't entirely trust. We were all alarmed amongst our little party. I was the only one without a passport and we were being marched at gunpoint back to our ship. My imagination was running riot and I was very afraid. I was desperate for a wee and terrified I might not last until I reached the safety of the ship. If I weed on the road as I walked I would be certainly clapped in jail.

To this day I remember catching sight of our purser sitting at a table at the quayside at the end of the gangplank joining Mexico to the safety of our home ship. He paid the manager the money we owed in the correct currency and I hurried to the loo and then our cabin, where our children were still awake. I cuddled them for hours until they got thoroughly fed up with me.

We had kept our cabin on B deck even though we had reached Acapulco. Probably no one wanted a cabin which had housed the mumps virus.

It was now Christmas and I filled my time answering a call from the children's nurse, who wanted any passengers to help with costumes and props for a performance of the Nativity to be held in the ship's theatre on Christmas Day. I spent my time making crowns, shepherds' crooks and angel wings. I was in my element, once more spending my time with children.

Next stop Lisbon, and nearly home.

CHAPTER 21

A HOMELY RAINBOW

As we neared Lisbon a mist appeared. My family were sleeping, so I quickly and quietly dressed and went up to A deck. I leaned on the rail and watched as Lisbon approached through the mist. I heard a foghorn – what a feeling! What an impact on my senses! The memory of it had an affinity to Dickensian murmurs of street lamps; double-decker buses, moors and the mills of my home town of Bradford flooded into my mind. I crept back to dress my children for our arrival in Lisbon. The ship's technicians had organised a phone line from the ship. I rang my home and my dad answered. My mum was at the shops, but the sound of my dad's voice was like pouring nectar on my head and shoulders. I hadn't spoken to him or seen him for four long years.

I loved my dad. He was the most philosophical and reassuring person I knew. I was safe.

I said, "I'm nearly home, Dad."

A day later I was in his arms. My mum and dad, Neil's parents, my brother and his wife and three boys and Neil's sister were in London to greet us. What was there to worry about? Indeed, all we had to do was find somewhere to live, schools for the children and, above all, work. With references like Neil's it seemed unlikely he would obtain employment in the field of physiotherapy, but luck was on our side. There was a huge postal strike in 1971–72. Neil contacted Philip, the former assistant principal of Otago Teaching Hospital, who saw only the good in Neil and thought he was a bit of a character – a maverick, but a useful physiotherapist. Philip was now teaching at Wolverhampton Teaching Hospital. Neil was offered a senior job even without references, simply on the strength of Philip's recommendation.

Philip was a very respected man and I had got to know him in New Zealand; he was a very professional and likeable character.

Neil was employed on a permanent contract, there was a good primary school for Linda and Christopher and I had applied for work through the Wolverhampton Education Offices. They seemed impressed with my credentials and offered me work. I had a choice, and it was a decision which deeply affected my future life. I could work in a special school, or a special unit attached to a secondary school, or teach English in a remedial department of a large comprehensive school.

Whilst I had been away in New Zealand, British schools had undergone a dramatic change. No longer were there grammar schools and secondary modern schools. Now these two methods of selection were no more. Now comprehensive education had been devised, where all children were educated on the same site with the same teachers and were studying the same subjects. According to the powers that be, no child should feel less than another. This policy intrigued me. In my mind, if all young people at secondary level were streamed into groups within one huge school, instead of two smaller ones, it would highlight the more academically challenged even more. So I opted for a new comprehensive school as my choice and was appointed to a high school on the outskirts of Wolverhampton as 'Lower School Head of Remedials'. We discovered a house for rent at Little Onn, which was a charming village with a shop, a church, and a pub which sold lunches in a basket. Nice.

The house was called Slab Bridge Cottage. Part of it dated to medieval times, with beautiful arched and mullioned windows, a double garage and extensive gardens adjoining the canal. Isolated, but utterly charming. The owners were away for one year, so this would suit me until my return to New Zealand.

Linda and Christopher were offered places in a school near to my new place of work, so we seemed relatively settled for at least one year.

CHAPTER 22

THE THREAT OF WASPS

I had been helped to get my introductions to the high school by an adviser to Wolverhampton's education authority who hadn't realised what an appallingly nervous driver I was. I had taken my driving test in Dunedin, where three cars in a row was deemed busy traffic.

When I had taken my test driving up and down the steep hills of the harbour, the examiner had said to me, "If I fail you, would you sit this test again?"

My reply was, "Yes, certainly – I will go on until I've passed."

"Oh," said the examiner, "in that case I'd better give you your pass certificate, because I couldn't go through that again!"

Now I was to follow the adviser in my second-hand Mini through the busy urban streets of Wolverhampton, where I was to deposit my children in their new school and then go on to my introduction to the head of my school and the head of the special-needs department. I drove with my heart thumping in my throat, hoping traffic lights wouldn't separate us and knowing that if I lost him I would simply stop my car and sit at the side of the road and cry with frustration.

We got to the school and the head obligingly allocated Linda and Christopher to two separate classrooms. The school was called Long Knowle Primary.

Linda, as always utterly charming, sat at a desk and smiled broadly at her new classmates. Christopher, on the other hand, was distraught and clung to me. It was terrible to leave him crying with his contorted tearful face pressed to the pane of glass in the classroom door. He was completely overwhelmed and my heart ached for having torn him away from all that was familiar. I went immediately to collect them following my interview and he was still upset and tearful. I had shaken my beautiful son's life to pieces; and as I drove back to Slab Bridge Cottage, getting hopelessly lost several times, I said, "Sorry, Christopher. I'm so sorry."

"Do I have to go back tomorrow?" he whimpered.

"Sorry, yes – that's your new school now."

Christopher said, "Will they still call me Danish Bacon?" Our surname was Denham and the boys in the class had distorted his name as a teasing nickname.

My heart was aching for him. He seemed inconsolable. But the next day he was up and ready and bravely got on with his life – something he has done ever since, and he makes me so proud of the way he makes himself face challenges and adversity. He is uncompromisingly brave, and I love him and admire his courageous and honest spirit. It has made me even more sensitive to the needs of children admitted to a school in midterm and without friends.

My appointment at the high school was now official and I was to become head of special needs in the lower school, dealing with K streams in the first three years of secondary education – streamed A–K (eleven streams). I was going to have to formulate some serious plans to deal with young people who deemed themselves at the very bottom of the pile.

A daunting but exciting challenge for me.

CHAPTER 23

A VERY COLOURFUL RAINBOW

We settled into a kind of routine. The days were counted off on my kitchen calendar towards my return to New Zealand. The murmur of an English springtime was in the air. The children seemed more settled. I loved my work and my word list of the progression of the English language was expanding and had taken on a very real shape helped enormously by working closely with the Experimental Literacy Programme organisation of Wolverhampton.

Now my life was to change irretrievably, dramatically and forever. I was about to meet the love of my life.

My plans for my return to New Zealand were forging ahead. I had to battle with the complexities of still living with my 'faraway' husband, whom I was tied to in my day-to-day life legally but not in any way emotionally or spiritually. We were sleeping in separate rooms and eating together with the children, but there was no other man-and-wife contact.

I had been working for three weeks in my new Wolverhampton school. I had a post-office box at Wednesfield Post Office, so I was able to keep in contact with my man in New Zealand, who was counting the days to my return.

I was sitting in the large staffroom of the lower

school chatting to my new friends and drinking my early morning coffee before school began. Through the corner door entered a man, and my heart missed a beat. I couldn't fathom out my own response. I'd never seen him before in my life.

I said, "Who is that?"

My neighbour replied, "That's Terry Miller. He's head of lower-school music. He's been off ill for a long time. He's always ill. He's quite a character, but he's got history."

That same day at break time he sat next to me. Heads were turning, and it was clearly apparent that there was chemistry and an attraction between us. I couldn't analyse or explain the feeling that I had landed where fate or destiny had meant me to be. One or two single women on the staff were clearly put out. I believe they had set their sights on this beguiling man. He was as thin as a stick, but seemed to give off powerful waves. He was an enigmatic and intriguing man, and I was ambushed by my own interest in him.

To add to his allure my K streams loved being with him for their music lessons. They would return from those music sessions with him with faces aglow, telling me of their exciting lesson with 'that Mr Miller'.

English, maths and humanities were spent with me, and they left the special-needs department only for music, PE, art and craft, and home economics – all of which they hated attending, except for music. I knew Terry must be giving them something of real value and not, like so many ex-grammar-school staff, giving them jobs to do which lowered their self-esteem and self-worth even more. They were often given the task of moving chairs ready for an assembly in the hall, picking up litter or tidying up bookshelves.

Terry made them feel worthy of being taught properly and worthy of being introduced to new things. I was impressed.

In the summer of that year I attended my high school's annual fête. I sat with my mum and dad, my two children and Neil. Terry was on the stage with his school orchestra and choir. He sat at the grand piano and appeared to be searching the audience. I was sitting three or four rows back with my family. He spotted me and winked. I melted, my heart beat faster and my legs felt weak. Neil spotted his wink and my reaction. He knew something was happening of importance. He stood and moved angrily along the row of seats to the exit. My loving intuitive and sensitive dad had also spotted the connection between us and got up in an effort to placate Neil.

They remained outside until the concert was over.

My dad took me by the arm and steered me around a corner – "Be careful, my girl. Neil is far from stupid and in his mind you are still his possession. He knows he has lost you, but he's not going to cope with your interest in another man. Take care – go to see a marriage counsellor. I am afraid for you, my girl."

But I wasn't afraid. I was simply flattered and excited.

CHAPTER 24

A SERIOUS WASP STING

I did take my dad's advice and did arrange meetings at the marriage-guidance offices in the centre of Wolverhampton. I went, then Neil went and then I went again. In that time Neil had become very jolly, as if he had sorted out the world's problems.

As I went into the offices of the guidance adviser, who was a very friendly, articulate middle-aged woman, she was smiling. Still smiling, she asked me to be seated. She spoke to me as if all problems were now solved and she had full explanations for my unhappy life with Neil. I heard with disbelieving ears words which might have helped me had I heard them ten years before.

"Your husband is a nice man. I'm sure you know that. He has told me he is an habitual masturbator, but when he performs these acts on himself it is always with your image in his mind. He is going to seek professional counselling and wants you to stay with him for the sake of the children. What do you think?"

"I think he is bloody bonkers. It is only now that he feels threatened by my departure that he is saying those awful words," I croaked in dismay.

There was no recognition or knowledge of what I had endured for a decade. The lies, the thieving, the laziness and the self-indulgent greed. I cried for the lack of sympathy and understanding. It was all too late. The thought of not being able to follow my instincts and nurture a relationship with a real man filled me with dread.

I went to bed that night in my separate bedroom at Slab Bridge Cottage. When it became light I saw my clothes had been moved around. My bra, which had hung on a chair, was now on my bedside table. Inside the cups were crosses – presumably meaning kisses – and a note saying, 'I love you.' I was horrified. He had been watching me whilst I slept.

I couldn't stay in that isolated house any more. Until I found some rented accommodation for myself and my children, my brother and sister-in-law and their three boys would come down from Yorkshire and stay with me. My dad encouraged this visit as he believed I was in great danger.

CHAPTER 25

A REAL RAINBOW

Again, my work in schools sustained me. I felt totally whole as I worked with children. The more disadvantaged they were, the harder I worked – offering myself completely, heart and soul, to their needs. I had developed a notion that became a realisation that the more disturbed and damaged a child was the more certain I had to be regarding their programme of study. Gone were the days when I admired kindly teachers who said, "Now then, children, what would you like to do today?"

There was to be a concert in the huge church at Wednesfield. I went along with my daughter, Linda, who was now nine and a half years old. On the stage was the entire school orchestra and a fifty-strong choir. On a podium, high on the balcony, was Terry, magnificent as he held the attention of the performers on the stage. I was mesmerised as he held each and every one of them in total silence and then raised his arms and conducted breathtakingly wonderful music, creative, positive and powerful.

Linda looked at me and said, "You like him, don't you, Mum?"

I replied, I don't know him that well, but I am going to find out about him."

What I found out was that this splendid man was suffering from depression. Sometimes it was so bad he couldn't work. His wife had attempted to get him sectioned. He had attempted suicide; he recovered from the attempt with his wife still wanting him out of her life, leaving her with the five children they had produced together in the home that Terry had built at Benter. He had gone off in a tiny caravan looking for work.

The more I got to know Terry, the more I wanted to be with him. My argument was if you share your life with a genius you have to put up with the flak and unusual behaviour.

The more I heard, the more I wanted to hear. I so wanted to be part of his life and near him. Terry was more and more involving himself with my less-able children at school. His honest interest was generous and comforting.

There was to be a pre-Christmas visit to an old people's home where Terry was responsible for the entertainment. He would take his singers, recorder players and drummers, and my special-needs children were to perform a little play.

I had always been drawn towards any child who seemed to have drawn the short straw when life's gifts were allocated. One small Year-8 girl had caught my attention. I loved her for her smile when she clearly had so little in her favour. Snotty and dirty, with unwashed hair, the same shirt all term and often no socks.

She was walking behind me with her best friend. They were both in my little play at the care home for the elderly; and as I was walking towards the care home with the school chaplain (who, regardless of protocol, thought Terry and I were a couple worthy of his backing), a little hand crept into mine and two bloodshot eyes looked up at me. It was Elsie, my favourite pupil, attired in dirty shirt but a new rather large blazer which had probably been provided by the school for this special visit.

"Do you like that Mr Miller?" she asked me.

"I don't really know him that well – but I like what I see," I replied, and Elsie wandered back to her friend, saying over her shoulder, "Me too."

A minute later back she came and into my hand once again came Elsie's hand. She looked at me as if she had lost all hope of obtaining Mr Miller for herself and said, "You do know you like him a lot, don't you, Miss?" And as a backhanded compliment she added, "I expect when you start shagging you'll have lovely children," and back to her friend she went.

The school chaplain was by now leaning on the entrance wall laughing almost hysterically. "How can you allow a child to talk to you like that?" he asked me.

"That's all she knows in her limited world – if you like 'em, shag 'em" was my reply – and into the care home we all walked.

Terry at the piano, recorders playing, the singers singing and my little play – the audience applauded. The children were smiling and then Terry stood up from his piano and beckoned me over. He said to the assembled residents of the care home, "I'm going to marry this lady as soon as I can."

I was reborn. Thoughts of a return to New Zealand vanished. I could not live without this man.

CHAPTER 26

WASPS STILL AROUND

A holiday travelling the canal in a long narrowboat had been planned for the summer of 1973. I no longer felt able to holiday with Neil; nor did I want to spoil a long-awaited adventure for my children.

Neil's dad said he would take the holiday with Neil and the children, and my brother Michael and his loyal wife and children would stay with me at Little Onn. Michael and Vivian, my wonderful sister-in-law, and Terry and I would go out for dinner on the first night we had the house to ourselves. It was a rather wet and stormy night. Neil had set off early in the morning, but I was anxious – particularly about Linda, who never ventured far from my side. At midday I had a phone call from Neil. He seemed surprised I was in. Would I take Linda's favourite toy to the canal lock gates on the other side of Wolverhampton? Vivian came with me in my little clapped-out Mini and we found them. I should have been more sensitive to Linda's distress and she clung to me as I handed over her favourite belongings. Christopher seemed content to run about on the barge, seemingly unaware of the tensions surrounding us. I should have gathered her up, but in my selfishness I was eager to get back to the cottage to get ready for an evening out and what I anticipated would be a rollicking night of fun and freedom. Terry was to arrive at 6 p.m. at the cottage and change from his work clothes into his Sunday best. We had booked a table for four at a rather posh pub/restaurant just on the outskirts of Cannock Chase. We had organised a fifteen-year-old babysitter who lived in the nearby village of Little Onn.

My beloved brother drove us and we ordered our meal. The first course arrived.

Terry stood up and said, "I feel something is wrong."

He went to the phone and rang Slab Bridge Cottage. He returned looking haggard and ashen-faced.

"We have to go back – there is something amiss at the cottage."

We paid the bill and drove back. It was still raining. As I opened the door the babysitter was in tears. Vivian and I were shaking. We were both mothers and our fears for our children must have been strongly evident in our distressed and worried faces.

Neil had travelled the canal at top speed, apparently rushing to catch me out in the company of Terry at the cottage adjoining the canal. Instead he had found an innocent babysitter and Michael's three boys asleep, but as he rampaged through the house he had discovered Terry's work clothes in the back room. Taking this as clear evidence of my infidelity, he had gathered up Terry's clothing, taken them outside and, screaming abuse, had thrown them in the deepest puddle of rain and jumped on them repeatedly.

We had tried to calm down the babysitter, but there were no words to reassure her. She thought she was trapped in an isolated cottage with a madman. Then I saw Christopher's frightened face at the window. Neil's dad, Neil and the children entered the house. Neil was completely out of his mind. He thought he was justified – I was still his possession and he had proof of my departure from my marital status.

My wonderful policeman brother remained calm. He drove the babysitter home to her very angry mother, who was rightly upset that her young daughter had been subjected to such a terrifying ordeal. Michael had wisely dropped off Terry on the way back from the restaurant at Birk's Barn Farm, where he lived with two bachelor friends in rented accommodation, four miles away down country lanes; so a very worried Terry was not witness to the mayhem.

Neil was ushering the children back to the barge, which was tied up at the bottom of the garden.

I said, "Don't take the children – let them sleep in their own beds. They are so tired and worried."

"No," said Neil, "they are my children. You are not a fit mother to care for my children."

My poor father-in-law was also very distressed, but could see no sense in dragging the children back to the barge.

"Let them stay in their own beds tonight. It's the kindest thing we can do now."

Neil and his dad went to sleep on their holiday barge a few yards away and I cuddled my children through the night. My nephews were sleeping in Linda and Christopher's beds, so my beautiful children and I crammed in together. I didn't sleep, but my brother was near. I always feel safer when he's around. What would I do without my brother? His steadying composure is always a lifeline. I knew I had to find myself a place to live. My dad was right: Neil was unstable and a dangerous threat.

It was all very clear to everyone observing Neil's behaviour that he had little or no self-control and he was a dangerous man.

CHAPTER 27

A HELPFUL RAINBOW

I not only had to find a home; I also had to find a solicitor. A wonderful understanding man with a practice in nearby Stafford was my chosen lawyer. He listened to my tale of woe and suggested I get out immediately and file for divorce. I was under threat and he would help me find a solution. I told Neil I was leaving him, but we would happily share the children at weekends and holidays.

"You can go – if you promise not to have anything to do with the music teacher," he said.

I promised. Would anyone ever believe that I promised this maniac that I would never see Terry again other than at our place of work?

I promised and lied and I convinced Neil that that was exactly what I would do. No Terry – what a bleeding hope that was!

I found a rented house in Sunley Drive, Hednesford, and Neil put private detectives on me to ensure I kept my promise to him.

To keep up appearances of propriety, Terry gave up his Birk's Barn Farm rented accommodation and moved into a room of a sweet old widow lady who lived on the main road out of Hednesford town, 300 yards away from Sunley Drive, where I was making my home. I toured junk shops in order to find some furniture to equip my little house. I had nothing except some bedding, my books and one or two treasures bought abroad. Terry had one suitcase, which contained a pair of blue sheets, a bread knife and his estranged father's glasses; and for some unknown reason he also had his father's false teeth!

Equipped for family life? Hardly!

Our year's tenancy at Slab Bridge Cottage had come to an end. Divorce was going ahead with much help and encouragement coming from my family. My dad and brother were also relieved, not only that I was going to live a separate life from Neil, but also that I did not intend to return to New Zealand.

Neil bought a house near to Linda and Christopher's school. My solicitor told me that Neil's advisers had suggested doing this in order to obtain custody of the children.

But then Neil made a major error in his judgement.

CHAPTER 28

I CAN HEAR THE WASPS

Linda and Christopher were taken away to Neil's parents' for the weekend. Neil had bought a snazzy red sports car which impressed Christopher no end. Linda was not so impressed. She forgave me much and felt safe near me. I am still in awe of her loyalty.

My dad was to pay for a phone to be installed into my new home, as much for his reassurance as mine, but it was not yet connected.

A policeman arrived at my door. He said, "Don't panic – your brother wants you to ring him."

"Is it my children? Are they hurt?" I shouted in his face.

The kindly policeman took my arm. "Don't panic – go to a public telephone and ring your brother. Your children are safe."

I rushed, barefoot, to the phone near the shop on Sunley Drive. My brother, Michael, answered the phone. He told me that Neil had gone to my parents' house in Bradford leaving Linda and Christopher in his car with his own parents. He had told my bewildered mum and dad that, because I had broken my promise to him about seeing Terry, I would never see my children again. He had proof of my lies with photographic evidence from the private detectives he had employed.

My dad said, "But, Neil, you are getting divorced from Julie. You can't take the children away – she is their mother."

Neil's reply was "She hasn't a chance now. She has proved herself capable of deceit and is not fit to call herself a mother. I am taking the children back to Wolverhampton today and they will stay with me forever."

Michael then told me I could drive over to Neil's house later that night, see the children and take some of their clothes and belongings.

To say I was distraught would be the understatement of all time. I was sick and very afraid. I could not live without my children; neither could I live without Terry.

My shakiest driving took place as I drove from Hednesford to Neil's home, where my precious children were, hoping they had arrived safely from Yorkshire. Michael had told me they had set off from Bradford straight after the visit to my parents' house. A terrible ordeal for them. My dad was holding his nerve, but according to my brother my mum was a distressed wreck – "always suffering from nerves", as she had always put it.

They had arrived at Neil's home and my wide-eyed and tearful Linda clung to me. Christopher was playing, but kept glancing at us, clearly moved by this horrible situation.

"Christopher wants to stay with me," said Neil – omitting Linda's name. Apparently she had been hard work and impossible to reason with despite many offerings of treats.

"What about Linda?" I asked.

"I'm going with Mummy," said my precious daughter, and then added, "I'll come back and see you, but I don't want to sleep here or have my breakfast here."

Neil would have had to physically tear Linda away from me. Something he wasn't prepared to do, especially with his parents there. Neil's dad was a kindly man. He had been head of science at a grammar school in Otley for many years before retirement and was now a town councillor. He was understandably uncomfortable; and perhaps I had imagined it, but I felt an energetic wave of sympathy for my awful situation transmitted to me.

I drove home with Linda pressed up against me and the steering wheel, but my heart ached for my son. I didn't see him for nearly four months, except occasionally when I dropped Linda off at the same school, when he would often catch sight of me and then dart off and hide. Heartbreaking.

Had I really lost my son to a dysfunctional madman? How could this be?

The pursuit of power with no links whatsoever to morality or someone else's peace of mind was so very strong in Neil. That was scary.

Would good sense and justice play a part in my future life?

CHAPTER 29

RAINBOWS COME AND GO

Most weekends Terry would visit his children. I had heard much about them: Andrew (the eldest), Ian, Tracey (who was about the same age as Linda), Alison (who was about Christopher's age) and then little Jonathan (who had only just turned three). I missed Terry, but I knew, so well, how important it is to be near your own children.

During the school holiday of 1973 Terry was taking Tracey to stay with his sister Sylvia in Doncaster, where she lived with her husband and three children. Sylvia had supported Terry's family throughout the troubled years leading up to the separation, and it seemed she would continue to do so.

On Terry's journey to Doncaster we had arranged to meet in a pub near Cannock, where I was to be introduced to Terry's firstborn daughter. My determination to successfully join my life to Terry's depended, I thought, on his five children liking me.

In the car park I spotted Terry standing with his nine-year-old daughter. The sun was bright, but there was a chill in the air and this painfully thin child was standing in a thin cotton dress smiling in my direction. She let go of her dad's hand, came towards me and took hold of my hand. All my instincts to protect and please a bewildered child surfaced. I loved her from that moment.

She said, "Dad says that the next school holiday I can come to your house with my brothers and sister and stay with you."

I replied, "That would be really lovely, Tracey. Are they all as nice as you?"

"I think so" was her innocent reply.

CHAPTER 30

SOMEWHERE NEAR THE WASPS ARE BUZZING

There was to be a divorce hearing at the Crown Court in Stafford. I was nervous and agitated and so fearful that my breathing was affected.

A social worker had visited me in Hednesford in order to arm the court with details about our lives. She had interviewed Linda alone and said to me how impressed she was with her honesty and her overall nature. I did not know about Christopher, as he had been interviewed in the company of his father and it had become clear that he was going along with whatever his father had instilled in his young mind. I was evil and unworthy to be his mother, Neil had told him.

My heart was breaking as I stood in court, visibly shaking and needing the toilet every few minutes.

The divorce proceedings were to go ahead, but custody decisions were complicated, according to the judge. He had said that there was something sadly amiss in the case and the custody hearing would be held separately at Birmingham High Court. Was this a hopeful sign? I would have to wait another month for that hearing to take place, but the divorce proceedings had begun.

CHAPTER 31

YET ANOTHER CLEAR RAINBOW

I was to meet four of Terry's children. It was a school holiday and I made preparations for their welcome using most of my limited income. Terry was paying a hefty maintenance amount for his five children and towards Rita's expenditures. They were all dependants, regardless of the fact that she had demanded her husband remove himself from her life. He was still responsible for her, so he couldn't help me financially at that time.

Mattresses were everywhere in my tiny rented home on Sunley Drive, but I had put surprises under their pillows and had a meal ready for them and plans to try and make them happy and comfortable.

Jonathan, the youngest, would not be with the other four. He was very young and got carsick very easily.

I had walked into Hednesford to buy four wooden stools I had seen in a junk shop; there were only two left when I got there. I carried them back along the main road to Sunley Drive. I already had four dining chairs, so we could take it in turns to eat if necessary. As I passed the large Hednesford Park on my left, I heard a hooting and a hollering behind me. It was Terry and his children waving frantically out of the car window. Ian and Andrew were giving me wolf whistles, which seemed a hopeful sign.

I had the most wonderful time with those precious children.

Andrew – so intelligent, amazingly so; Ian with his generous skills of appeasement; Tracey, whom I'd met, desperate to please and full of ideas for little plays and songs to keep us all amused; and dear Alison, the sweet innocent, who in her effort to please would say "Still is" if someone said a meal was nice; Jonathan, whom I met at a later date, charmed everyone with his blond hair, blue eyes and the face of an angel. How lucky I felt to think I might be part of their lives.

CHAPTER 32

WASPS EVERYWHERE

To add to my fears of losing my children I found I had a very real problem with Terry's drinking habits.

It was becoming apparent that there were many demons in his head. As his history unravelled I began to appreciate how difficult his growing-up years had been for him. He not only had to contend with an extremely controlling mother, whose expectations and demands amounted to a form of bullying – this was verified by his aunts and uncles – but he was evacuated at the age of eleven and very much left to fend for himself. From all accounts, the task of maintaining himself rested on his own young shoulders. It seems there were none of the comforts you might expect from adults who knew he was separated from his family. He guided himself, but it seems that, without emotional support and spiritual guidance, by the time he was appointed to the post of radio operator on naval minesweepers at the tail end of the war he became largely dependent on alcohol to settle his troubled mind.

When I objected or showed concern or alarm, Terry became fiercely defensive and sometimes angry. However, his strengths in every other direction were so impressive that I tried to squash down my fears and the feeling of loneliness which materialises when one person in a couple is sober and the other drunk. Never in my life had I met someone so talented and so skilful. He could even knit. He told me one day he had won competitions not only for music and dancing, but also for knitting.

"Is there no bloody thing you can't do, Mr Smart-arse?" was my question.

I had to eat my words when we visited his Aunty Alice in Walthamstow, East London. When I met her for the first time she opened the door to us and asked, "Have you won any more knitting competitions lately, Terry?"

Whatever my worries about Terry's need for copious amounts of alcohol, I loved him dearly. Not only did I want to be with him, I wanted to have his baby. To have a child with someone you really love must be a wonderful thing, I thought.

Crazy idea really. Terry had five children and I had two. Really crazy, but the desire was there in my mind and I couldn't budge it.

Neil's plots to derail us were manifested time and time again. He even rang my bank manager at Lloyds and told him I was not to be trusted; then he put that alarming story in writing to the head office of Lloyds. He even wrote to the head of Wednesfield School and told him that Terry had propositioned sixth-form girls and had sexual relationships with those girls in the school grounds. Neil stopped at nothing to deliver blow after blow with stinging power at Terry and me. This was particularly harmful to me as my career was looking so promising. I had been entrusted with more and more responsibilities, and my reputation for restoring self-esteem and purpose was strong and healthy.

But fate was going to turn the tables on Neil.

CHAPTER 33

RAINBOWS IN SIGHT

The day arrived when the custody hearing was to be held in Birmingham High Court. I sat in the waiting room being briefed by my wonderful solicitor, Mr Durell.

He said, "I am told by Neil's solicitor that Neil will claim that you made impossibly excessive sexual demands on him. Lucky sod!"

"Gosh," says me, "is once every eight years excessive?"

"He is also going to say that Christopher does not want to be with his lying, cheating mother."

That statement threw me utterly and completely, and as I stood in the dock I felt faint and nauseous. How could anyone not believe me that I had managed for years in very difficult circumstances and I had always done my very best for my children?

The Judge looked at me and I felt safer. He was looking at me with understanding. My solicitor told me later that the Judge would have read all the affidavits from New Zealand and would have realised what kind of a human being Neil was.

The Judge said, "Well now, Mr Denham, I am told you are applying for an interim custody order for your two young children. Is this correct?"

Pure arrogance oozing from Neil's countenance, he replied "Yes, M'Lord. That is correct."

"Then why are you applying for an interim order when you have already taken the law into your own hands and kept your son from his mother?"

Neil's reply was, "He doesn't want to be with his mother."

The Judge said, "Seven-year-old boys do as they are told. You must return him at once to his mother and you will pay maintenance. You have caused severe pain to your family and they don't deserve such treatment."

My solicitor had told me that eventually good sense would prevail, but this was an unexpected turn of events and pure delight. Wise people had seen through the murk and mire of our troubled lives. My steadfast brother and sister-in-law were in attendance as usual. We tried to celebrate, but Linda was ill in bed in Hednesford with only a neighbour keeping an eye on her; so we couldn't conga round Birmingham as we all wanted to, but we all felt much, much better.

CHAPTER 34

WASPS HOVERING AGAIN

Neil was to meet me at a roundabout on the Hednesford Road and hand Christopher over to me. Neil's face was florid and angry-looking. I felt sorry that it had come to such a distressing point for all of us, but I was overjoyed to be able to have my son near me again.

As I drove back to my little home, I could see Christopher, with arms folded defiantly, looking grim as he sat in the back seat. He looked so unapproachable when all I wanted was to cuddle him.

I made tea and Christopher ate in silence, so different from my happy, carefree, outgoing son. He sat unspeaking until bedtime. He climbed into bed and immediately fell asleep. I suspect he wanted to shut out the world and his worries. I went to bed about 10.30 p.m., but couldn't resist the urge to look at him and treasure the fact that he was home with me. I bent to kiss his forehead and his eyes opened wide. Only horror was demonstrated in his tormented stare.

"Go away," he said. "My dad says you're a witch and he'll dance on your grave."

I staggered downstairs and cried like I'd never cried before or since. I was broken, completely shaken to the core. What had we done to this beautiful boy? His mind was truly poisoned and I didn't know how to mend it.

How could a mother suddenly not be a mother? He was my precious, beautiful son. How had I ruined his life?

I had received a legal letter stating that the house in Sunley Drive did not actually belong to the people we were renting it from and I had one month to vacate the property. Also adding to my dilemma, Mr Hart, the adviser for special needs in Wolverhampton, was so impressed with my work that he was offering me the headship of a new purpose-built school for children with special educational needs.

"You have the qualities to make it sing," he told me.

I had to decline. I told him that my life was in such chaos at the moment that I would never do it justice. He gave me a hug and wished me luck.

Terry's humour often rescued me. I was a bit of a poser. On one occasion I was out on the field at school taking a cover or substitute lesson for an absent colleague knowing full well that Terry could see me from his second-floor music-room window. I made wild and authoritative gestures just to impress as I made up new rules for a rounders match.

"Did you see me out on the field, Terry?" I said later in the staffroom.

"Indeed I did," said Terry. "Who could miss that fat arse?"

Once when I was driving along I was waxing lyrical about the sunset reflected in windows. "It's like watching the sunset over Tahiti reflected in my ship's windows."

"Ships have portholes, not windows," said Terry.

"F--- off," I said completely put down.

But eventually we got the measure of one another and we forgave each other our flaws.

CHAPTER 35

A RAINBOW REAPPEARS

My children were now in my care. I could now decide how I was to make them feel safe and happy.

Terry's divorce was finalised, as was mine. We would marry and move nearer to Terry's children. With the help of Terry's Aunty Alice, his Uncle Joe and Uncle Joe's son, known as Joe Boy, who all lived in and around London, we would marry in Walthamstow. My parents would come and my brother and sister-in-law and Terry's sister and husband and as many of our now seven-children family as we could fit into the car.

We had seen work advertised in the *Times Educational Supplement* for two teachers in a school for the maladjusted in Bath, which is only a bus ride from Benter, where Terry's children lived with their mother.

My teaching adviser said that he wouldn't touch such work with a bargepole. If the head of that school was an advocate of 'acting out' methodology any teacher would be doomed. But the school, known as Wansdyke School for Maladjusted – a cruel name – suited us in every other way, so we applied. My dear friend and colleague, Sue Etienne, offered to care for my two children when we were called for interview.

The school consisted of several Nissen-type

Terrapins with a large hall. There was also a permanent glazier because of the frequency of smashed windows. We did not think this was a good sign, but we were interviewed and we were both appointed to work in that school. One of the jobs was permanent and the other temporary, so we were going to face a difficulty at a later stage, but we could move nearer to Terry's children. Our accommodation was sorted for us by one of the school governors, who also had links with the Admiralty Housing Committee. We were offered a top flat at 23 The Circus, Bath. Many stairs, but a large flat as it covered the stairwell and had been the servants' quarters in wealthier times gone by.

We moved; we settled in. No washing machine, no fridge or freezer – just a lot of steps and the Lansdown pub round the corner, which suited Terry. He went every single night and lunchtimes too during the holidays, but I kind of got used to it.

We were planning the wedding for 26 January 1974 in Walthamstow. I worked and planned, and Terry worked and planned and drank. Terry's children came each weekend, and now I found I was expecting Terry's baby in May, not long after our planned wedding.

A few happenings arose which caused us amusement as well as headaches. Our car was an old heap and kept stalling on the way to our wedding. We took three of Terry's children and my two. We left Andrew (the oldest) and Jonathan (the youngest) with Hilda, their mother, and every time the car broke down the seven of us had to unravel ourselves from the car and push it until it bump-started itself into action again. Christopher kept moaning about missing *Doctor Who* – and Terry had booked me into what he thought was an hotel, but actually was a registered home for battered wives!

The register-office wedding was lovely. I wore a

cream maternity dress and stuck as many flowers in my hair as I possibly could, to form a distraction from my rapidly growing tummy.

Terry had organised the reception in a lovely London pub and everyone was positive and happy for us, except when Terry's brother-in-law surprised us by saying he wished us luck but he thought the whole venture was a big mistake and heading for disaster.

But we proved him wrong. It has been the most exciting, tumultuous, mind-blowing, adventurous and glorious marriage of all time.

CHAPTER 36

NOW MAINLY RAINBOWS WITH VERY FEW WASPS AROUND

On 29 May 1974 our baby girl was born. She was beautiful and she was safe. I have a fear of hospitals, possibly arising from being isolated in a fever hospital at the age of five. My mother had attributed the scarlet fever to my waywardness as I had been eating the icicles which hung from the drainpipes of our frozen roof. I couldn't understand this idea, because I had been the Ice Queen and that was all she ate and she hadn't caught scarlet fever. A reasonable eating habit for an ice queen, I thought.

I had both Linda and Christopher at home and I intended to have my third baby in my own bed in my own way. The hospital authorities were adamant that this was inadvisable for an elderly primate – a term I had been given owing to my great age (I was thirty-six). It was also considered inadvisable for a baby to be born in a top flat with no modern facilities, lots of children and no lift.

"Totally impractical and dangerous," said the doctor at St Martin's Hospital. "What if the health of you or your unborn baby is under threat? What if emergency services have to be called?"

My wonderful and wise midwife came to my rescue. "Julie has a fear of hospitals. Her blood pressure is high now because she is being assessed in a hospital. When I take her blood pressure at home, she is fine."

So with the cooperation of Dr Speer, who was willing to see me through my pregnancy, and Sister Lowe I was safely delivered of my precious baby girl in the top flat of 23 The Circus, Bath.

All was well.

Six weeks after the baby was born I returned to work. We had a nanny, but life had many stresses. It wasn't as if work in a special school was easy and straightforward. I have always felt, very deeply, that the more damaged and disturbed a young person is, the more certain you have to be in how you conduct your lessons; but this was not the system in this school, so I was flying in the face of a procedure which I wasn't at all comfortable with. It seemed to annoy the head that the pupils enjoyed being with me. Staff meetings became a battle of wits, and both Terry and I began looking for other schools, where more rigorous standards were in place.

Terry would relieve stresses by visiting the pub, but baby-bedtime, homework, shopping and preparing lessons were beginning to take their toll on me and my already short fuse became even shorter; even the smallest mishaps would throw me into an uncontrollable tizzy.

Wednesday nights were the hardest because we had to stay after school for an extra hour to talk about our work. We had to make contingency plans. Christopher would walk from Beechen Cliff School, Linda would go with her friend Rebecca to her house and meet us later, and the nanny would bring Sarah an hour later than usual. To avoid having to make a late meal we would pick up fish and chips on the way home. Problem solved.

One particular Wednesday we got back to the flat with everyone's meal wrapped up in newspaper. I sat Sarah in her high chair, got out salt and vinegar and tomato sauce and sat down to enjoy my ready-made meal.

Terry looked at me with raised eyebrows and said, "Where's the bread and butter? You know I can't eat fish and chips without bread and butter."

Again I lost all my self-control. "How unfair!" I said. "It's not my f------ job to go shopping as well. I've worked all f------ day, just like you, you f------ chauvinist pig!" and I threw all the fish and chips on to the floor and proceeded to jump on them. I had nothing on my feet, so the fish and chips were squashing up between my toes; and as the children choked with laughter, I screamed out, "Is there no justice in the world?"

We went to bed hungry that night. Terry brought us all crisps, pickled eggs and nuts back from the pub, but the children had gone to bed and had only eaten cold baked beans from the tin.

Christopher said the next day, "Don't cross my mother – she gets pretty mad when she's upset."

I have to point out that during my professional development Terry's drinking plagued me often. In fact, when Sarah was very small I wheeled her round in her pram to the pub where her dad was enjoying his daily consumption of Guinness, pushed my way in and said loudly, "This is where your dad lives," and walked out again to loud laughter from the pub dwellers.

Gradually we cut one another some slack, and our appreciation of each other's strengths took over. It took over completely with only the very occasional hiccough.

It seems to me that you can cope with problems if you are happy in some aspect of your life. If your spirit is content, difficulties diminish.

Both Terry and I were struggling with a school system which suited neither of us. Terry was interviewed for the headship of the Stage V Centre in Bath. There were three new centres to be set up in the area, with one in Weston-super-Mare and the other in Bristol. These centres would accommodate young people who were finding difficulty coping with the demands and expectations of secondary education. There were to be five stages of expulsion from mainstream school and the Stage V Centre was to be their final stage of exclusion. Terry was ideally suited to this work. He had coped brilliantly teaching on the Isle of Dogs in the East End of London, and his clear and deliberate attitude would stand him in good stead.

Terry was appointed as the head teacher of the Bath Stage V Centre. We were delighted, but it left me alone at Wansdyke School for Maladjusted in work I didn't relish.

But I learned much and found that the painstaking planning of the detail of my lessons made life easier for me, and I stood my ground with my methods. But it wasn't easy. It always felt like I was emptying the bath with a spoon. I now knew, positively and unmistakably, what my teaching skills were. I could tell stories in such a way that I was able to grab a young person's attention. By quietly listening to their stories and giving them my rapt interest I could give children focus and a belief that their lives were truly important, and I could offer them something to do which they recognised as valid. I could ascertain within moments a child's level of ability and gear their work appropriately – within reach, but stretching them to a further step on the educational ladder. I could also make each enterprise fun by inventing appropriate games geared to the child's coping capacity. I had also learned when to give moments of silence and solitude when reflection could occur and then make ready for the next stage. If a child left my room unsmiling and not eager to return, I knew I had failed.

I had to find work where my skills could be better used. There was an advert in the educational bulletin requiring English-language teachers at the newly opened Multicultural Centre in Bristol. I applied and was offered the post of ESL (English as a second language) teacher, Scale 3, but peripatetic, which meant I went from school to school offering help where teachers were being faced with non-English speakers. I didn't tell them that I was a nervous driver and had never driven through Bristol!

But this work was my salvation. It had every component to satisfy my teaching and learning style and ticked every box in my need to reach bewildered and often frightened young people. I was rejoicing.

My first two schools were Lockleaze School and the Rose Green Annexe of St George School. The latter became my base for the next twenty-five years because the catchment included so many children from immigrant and asylum-seeking and refugee families. I was in my element and looked forward to every single moment in schools. Life seemed rich and fulfilling. Terry was succeeding well with his Stage V Centre and was much respected for his clear leadership and no-nonsense approach. All our children seemed well and happy, with some of them achieving great things academically – particularly Andrew, who eventually got to study at Brasenose College, Oxford.

Now everything seemed to be in place for a good life. We moved from the top flat in Bath to a tiny village, three miles away, called Corston, where Terry quickly became 'king' with his exceptional organisational skills and his charismatic nature.

My work was endlessly satisfying. It felt as if fate had steered me into the most rewarding and fulfilling field of work. My graded word lists were complete and printed. They were much sought after by teachers who had witnessed the strategy and were willing to control the movement from card to card, but not so successful if teachers were left to work the system out for themselves. The box containing the graded cards was now called 'Strategy to Fluency'.

Terry's drinking habits often taxed and frustrated me, but my work was solidly satisfying. I made tape recordings of the sentences so the children could hear the missing word and select the correct one from the list. This gave me reassurance that they were not simply 'barking at print'; they were listening to the English words in context.

Ken Reeves was the head of the Multicultural Centre in Bristol and heaped praise on the success of my teaching. Unknown to me he sent descriptions and samples of my methodology to the College of Preceptors. This was the college responsible for awarding both Terry and me with associate membership when we worked in Wolverhampton.

This college was the professional teaching body responsible for scrutinising teaching methods, historically dating back to the dame schools towards the end of the nineteenth century. They were responsible for the standardisation of teaching methods and offering certificates and awards for samples of good teaching practice.

To my amazement and delight I was awarded a fellowship. I was now a Fellow of the College of Preceptors and named as having made an outstanding contribution to education. I was over the moon with excitement and delight. To add to the glory, I was then asked to present a paper at an educational-research conference in Monastir in Tunisia, all expenses paid.

'I've made it,' thought I. 'There's no stopping me now. My fame will spread worldwide.' I was on the edge of cockiness and big-headedness.

My wonderful dad had to remind me to keep my feet on the ground. I don't know of any teachers who became famous. Don't stick your head so far up your own arse that you can't see anything," he said.

Good advice, but I remained lofty right up until I stood on the platform of a huge Islamic hall facing a roomful of academics. It was then I went to pieces and everyone witnessed my knocking knees and my trembling hands. I couldn't hold my notes.

Somehow I was rescued. It was God holding my hand yet again. I had to be truthful – I was not an academic. I was singularly out of my depth and had to be honest and said, as I held my head high, "I feel utterly fraudulent. I am just an ordinary teacher who happens to love my job. But I have learned one important lesson during my career so far and that is that human beings have an infinite capacity to hurt one another but we also have an infinite capacity to make each other feel good. Sadly many of us choose the former and think that by pushing someone down we somehow lift ourselves up. It is a see-saw attitude. I believe that the worst thing we can do is make another person feel of no consequence. For instance, if we are waiting in our car to join a main road and no one lets us in to join the traffic we often get irritated – even angry – not because we are in a hurry but because we have been made to feel of no consequence."

At this point a large bearded man at the back of the hall stood up and began to applaud. A few other people joined him in the clapping.

I said smilingly, "You have done exactly what I have been stating. You have made me feel as if I have something of value to contribute."

I put down my notes and simply spoke about the many actions we can undertake to make an unhappy or lonely person feel worthwhile, and I gave examples of the many refugee children who had endured horrendous experiences but have been helped towards a happier future. I spoke for over my allocated time of thirty-five minutes. I couldn't have been utterly boring or worthless because I was asked to present a paper the following year, this time in Ibiza, and my discarded notes were published in *Education Today*, a monthly publication for teachers with worldwide readership.

My work in schools was developing into an acceptable strategy. Graduates hoping to go on to teaching were sent to me in huge groups. The work had become solidly satisfying for me as I had now put into place not just a clear programme taking children from nowhere to somewhere quite quickly. I was able to put forward to any willing listeners what I believed to be four necessary components or requirements towards creating an ideal EAL (English as an additional language) teacher:

1. To be able to assess levels of English language competency at the speed of light. A good EAL

teacher will accept that a new student may be too embarrassed to show his/her limited English when an interpreter is explaining the circumstances of the student being admitted on to the school roll. A student being rated as a non-English speaker may have a good grasp, an excellent grasp or no grasp whatsoever in the quiet non-threatening atmosphere of an intimate EAL room.

2. To offer a programme with an incline of difficulty woven into it which allows you, the teacher, to offer purposeful pursuits regardless of English language skills, and a clear step-by-step skills ladder towards progress.

3. To throw the whole weight of your personality into this systematic approach, to be clearly overjoyed – and in my case, noisily jubilant – that a child can recognise your approval even if it is only for having made a circle with a pencil when the pupil is from a nomadic background and has never made a recognisable symbol on a surface before and is therefore illiterate in any language.

4. To have been hurt in your personal life, so you, the teacher, are aware and sensitive to the painful memories registering in the eyes and demeanour of the child you are dealing with. To accept that this is a very hurt, very bewildered and very lost young person who needs you to take him/her to a place of safety and comfort, where learning can take place, is essential. I find it a useful ploy to register an apologetic attitude for not understanding their language rather than irritation or frustration that they are not able to understand mine.

CHAPTER 37

CREATING MY OWN RAINBOWS

My first Somali pupils were all male. Most of them had travelled northwards from the horrors of war to the refugee camps in Ethiopia. The British consul, the Red Cross and immigration officials had done a fine job of containment and rescue. Young males between the ages of eleven and sixteen were put on to planes provided they had a sponsor in Britain. These sponsors were invariably students, often penniless, but could offer food and shelter and very little else to these young refugees who had frequently lost some or all of their family members.

Many of these children would often arrive at school quite hungry. From choice they had decided they would not be a burden to their new protectors and would wait for the school meal served to them free of charge at 12.30 p.m.

Oh, the awesome strength of Islam.

I decided I could use food as a reward system in my work and avoid giving them a feeling of accepting charity or pity. These proud young people would not have willingly accepted charity. My method also gave me the measure of their English-language acquisition without it being apparent to anyone but me.

I would put on my table an array of goodies. This

system did not work well during Ramadan, when they were fasting, but they could build up a nest egg or take success cards to build up a later store of treats. The array would usually consist of apples, oranges, drinks, potato crisps and chocolate.

At the 'no English at all' level the pupil would point to what they would like after gaining the necessary points. I would indicate that at thirty points they could choose one thing. They would point and gain the food object of their desire. At the 'some English' level they would say the word of their selection. But the moment I knew they had made the journey to English-language mastery would be when they said, "Well, actually, Miss, I wondered if you had any prawn-cocktail crisps left and are they halal?" (Acceptable food for all who follow Islam.)

There were so many 'Damascus moments' when I discovered the history of some of my pupils – moments which changed my attitude to the inhabitants of this world forever. All human beings have their stories to tell, but some are more soul-numbing than others.

Whilst working at St George School in Bristol, now known as the City Academy, I received my first Somalis. The deputy head at the time liked the way I worked and frequently sang my praises.

One particular day he said to me, "I am bringing you two Somali brothers. They witnessed the hanging of both their parents outside their school in Mogadishu. If you can't do anything with them, nobody can."

I was truly humbled and didn't know quite what to expect. I was fully aware that my skills were hardly sufficient to cope with young people who had experienced such horrors.

It was clear that the younger brother was coping well with his new life in Bristol, but the older one's smiles were hard to come by. He stayed in my room most of the school day. He was a great cricketer and joined in some PE sessions, but not all. There were moments of refusal and he would sit with his head in his hands immobile for several minutes.

I read him some simple stories and showed him illustrations and photographs that I thought might bring forward a smile. One morning I showed him a picture of a family on a camping holiday. The mother figure was cooking over a campfire. When I looked at my boy, the tears were rolling down his face. I took his hand in mine and put the picture away – as far away as possible – without losing my hold on his hand. He put his damp face on mine and looked at me.

"Sorry," said I, "I am silly. That is not a good picture for you."

The boy said, "Thank you. You know, you know, you know. I am sad."

It was nothing and it was everything. He trusted me.

The following day he fell off his chair twice. The second time he banged his head on a bookcase quite severely. I sent for my trusted deputy head, who sent for the young brother, who had marginally more spoken English than his older brother. The young brother pulled up the trouser leg of his sibling, and there on his legs were untreated shrapnel wounds. The shrapnel had penetrated muscle and bone and the skin was growing over the appalling wounds. I was told his bloodstream was being poisoned. He must have been in great pain throughout his days in the Ethiopian camp, the escape northwards, his journey here and all the time I had been teaching him. What courage and endurance! And now he was looking at me apologetically as if he was sorry for being a trouble; and as he got into the car to be taken to hospital, he said sorry – to me!

I was told he thought his mother was alive after she had been hanged because he saw her feet move.

This and other tales of brave spirits enduring against the odds came to my attention, and there were many times when I had to pull off the road between school and home because I could not see the road clearly enough through my tears.

My classroom or teaching area had been the old home-economics area: two large rooms with bays containing cookers, work surfaces and sinks. One of my new Somali students refused to remove his anorak and hood. I had accepted this as a sign of insecurity and I made no comments, but more worrying behaviour did bother me. Every five or six minutes this boy would go to a sink, fill the washing-up bowl with water and then proceed to splash his face. I thought at first he was unused to running water.

After several weeks of water splashing I went to my deputy-head mentor, who listened to me attentively then sent for some Somali students who were studying at Bath University. They duly arrived and took my pupil into a quiet office. I sat outside waiting for an explanation for this bizarre behaviour.

After about twenty minutes one of the university students came out and said, "Are you Mohamed's teacher?"

"Yes," I said. "Can you tell me why Mohamed keeps splashing his face with water?"

The student's reply was "Mohamed is trying to get the smell of dead bodies out of his nose."

I was shaken out of any complacency. I just wanted to mend this broken world. My heart actually ached. A physical pain in me caused by another's suffering. My determination grew as my heart and mind took on case after case of young people blighted by adults who did not see some human beings as worthy of any respect or care.

One boy had been bashed so hard on the head his optic nerves were damaged beyond repair; another boy was so traumatised by war he had lost the power of speech; and one young Afghan had lost his entire family in the big snows of 2012. He had freakishly been elsewhere when his village was snowed in and frozen.

Humbled as I was, my determination grew. My whole mind was now focussed on bringing hope, life and laughter to these young people. Instead it became *they* who inspired me to greater efforts. I discarded most advice and protocol. I would do whatever necessary to create a working space for my precious children so they could focus on the assignments I gave them and I would positively reinforce every scrap of progress with high praise, parties, laughter and chocolate.

The very first time one of my pupils tasted chocolate I thought I was observing a triple orgasm – not that I know personally what that experience is like – it is only what I have had described to me!

I now used every trick in the book and more to make learning English an enjoyable and exciting experience, and it was working in a better way than I ever anticipated.

I was very fortunate that my school allotted me space to take small groups of individuals when the need arose and when real trauma was detected.

I was so very lucky. Most staff were admiring of the students' progress, but not all. I heard sometimes that a teacher was envious of my small classes, but I was working harder than I'd ever worked in my entire life.

But it was so good when I was trusted – and sometimes even loved.

CHAPTER 38

A KIND OF WASP EXPERIENCE

Now I was heading towards sixty years of age and Terry nearing seventy. He had retired ten years earlier and was now a truly valuable member of the village. Terry was on every committee. He was clerk to the village council, chief organiser of clubs and trips out for the older members of the community, and constantly on the move. He was also a consumer of a great deal of alcohol, but he was much admired and his advice and helpfulness was sought after. His walking became limited, and in 2003, when we were all consumed by the notion of war in Iraq, his knees failed him. His left knee was particularly troublesome. The doctor said that he needed a knee replacement and X-rays confirmed this necessary treatment. The NHS had an impossibly long waiting list, but if Terry was willing to travel overseas the NHS would foot the bill. I could go with him, but I, of course, would not be NHS-funded.

The week before the Iraq War began we were in La Clinique Pasteur in St-Étienne in the South of France. Terry would stay the full three weeks, but I would return to the UK after ten days because of my school commitments. To travel alone from a foreign airport filled me with dread, but the time I had with Terry was so very worthwhile. He had wine with his meals

– non-drinkers were donating their bottles to him, acknowledging his liking for the stuff, and his room often smelt like a brewery. His single room housed his bed, a wall-mounted television, a fold-up bed with a lumpy mattress for me and an orthopaedic chair. It had a tiny shower room and toilet en suite and, wonder of wonders, a balcony where I could have a cigarette. Joy of joys!

The nurses were utterly splendid, and doctors and surgeons beyond brilliant. The care was outstanding and the interpreter was so kind and helpful it was enough to make me weep. She became a real friend and later visited us at home in Corston with her English husband.

The time came for me to leave Terry. A taxi was to pick me up at the hospital and take me to the tiny airport at St-Étienne. I had charged my phone and had made arrangements for my son Christopher to meet my plane at Stansted.

As I disembarked from the plane, stressed beyond belief, I rang his mobile number. He answered straight away.

"I'm here," says me.

"I know – I can see you, Mum."

My shoulders went down and my love for my son soared skywards. My dear, dependable, adorable son. Who could ask for more?

He drove me to his home in Milton Keynes – a large four-bedroom detached house – but rather than remove one of his three children from their own rooms, he gave me his big double bed and he and Glenys, his wife, slept downstairs on sofas. They knew I ached for comfort and space and peacefulness. Then Christopher drove me home and stayed with me until the next day, and then drove back to his family. But then, to avoid the emptiness I was feeling, Linda stayed nights until I could be reunited with Terry.

My wonderful, steadfast, loving children. I felt truly whole when Terry was once again by my side.

Terry could walk again without pain. He used a stick, but he looked magnificent in his brown corduroy suit, his fedora or straw hat and his smile, which lit up my world.

CHAPTER 39

DEFINITELY A RAINBOW

I must have been to hundreds of in-service days during my career, and in just about each and every one I've felt so bored and disconnected. I'd be watching the clock for a coffee break and thinking, 'Oh, God, my bum is going to be on this hard chair for the next two hours'– except for one which I attended at Bishopston Teachers Centre many years ago.

A woman had come to talk to us about portage – a system of moving a human being along a step-by-step route on an educational and progressive ladder.

As I listened I felt so very comfortable. This is what I had been instinctively doing so far in my teaching life, and here was someone putting a name to it and giving it a description and a validity. I thought, 'I'm not going to make excuses for the way I behave in the classroom.' Here was a professional putting into clear words a method I knew worked. I was overjoyed and wanted to hug this very articulate and enthusiastic woman.

She made it sound so simple and workable. Yet there were still so many teachers who were asking children to copy out pages from textbooks and copy diagrams, praising them for neatness when understanding was completely absent from the learning process.

Portage is accepting a goal as your objective. But success was not dependent on reaching that end goal. The achievement and the success is built into each tiny step towards that goal. For instance, a child with a disability might have a problem putting on his shoes. Each task was written down which built up towards the end target. In this case, the steps might be:

- Place foot by shoe – success.
- Place foot on shoe – success.
- Place foot in shoe – success.
- Fasten buckle – success.
- Walk on shoe – success.

The end target reached is not the biggest success. Each step needs praise and is an achievement in itself, regardless of the end target. This is the way I worked and wanted to work forever.

It was with such delight I left that assembly of teachers. I would stick to my step-by-step programme, where children felt good about their efforts however limited or humble the task.

One of my nomadic pupils from Somalia knew all about which grasses camels could eat or not eat and which caused the animals to become violent. But he had never made a mark on a surface to represent an order or script, so when he held a pencil and could make a circle where the beginning met the end I rejoiced and shouted, "Muse Khahin for king!" and clapped until my hands hurt. He hadn't learned to write, but he'd reached the first vital stage of literacy. Each stage is celebrated noisily – in fact, as noisily as any final stage of accomplishment. Each and every tiny step would be set down on a programme so a pupil could highlight each completed step and actually see their own individual progress. Psychologically this is a profound advantage. They compare each other's highlighted progress. Not only that, but they can see their starting point and what else is in front of them. Invariably this has a positive effect on a person's need to feel they are progressing towards a common aim. That is literacy and fluency in their new language. It has to be noted that teaching English as a foreign language is vastly different from teaching English as a second or additional language. With EFL you are usually instructed in your home language and the urgency is virtually non-existent. But with EAL the pupil is in school or college having to access the curriculum in the new language. They are having to go from subject to subject without having the tools of understanding of each subject's individual vocabulary. It is unlikely that a pupil who has no understanding of what scaffolding is, because he has no experience of a building site, will understand osmosis or the transmission of neutrons. To add to the complexities of new-language acquisition, African, Asian and Arabic scripts are not rooted in Greek or Latin, as are many, or even most, European languages. Punctuation, spaces between words and the use of small and capital letters are also hurdles to overcome.

To weave these script obstacles into a pupil's learning has to be a positive undertaking without showing one's own exasperation at the enormous tasks which lie ahead.

Identifying the new task then simplifying it is absolutely essential to the well-being of a first-stage English-language learner. We must never leave a pupil feeling the way forward is fraught with difficulties or feeling awestruck at what lies ahead.

I learned that a teacher can shrivel up a child's confidence and feelings of well-being in a millisecond by a look, a gesture, eye rolling, clicks of the tongue or just a turning away of a head and in an instant undo any progress which might have been made previously.

We must never underestimate the power of body language, and, even more importantly, remember that for a person who is not familiar with their new language, gestures are read at the speed of light.

My work in schools, with bewildered and often frightened young people, continued to flourish and at lightning speed. I was managing to earn respect for the unusual methods which I had adopted in order to dispel the feelings of hopeless inadequacy which prevailed in so many of my students.

CHAPTER 40

MOST DEFINITELY A RAINBOW

Terry had an Aunty Audrey who was roughly the same age; and although she was the sister of Terry's mother, she grew up with Terry as if they were cousins. She adored Terry, and Audrey's husband, Sid, was a very great admirer of all Terry stood for and had accomplished. The highlight of Sid's life, every three months, was to receive an edition of the *Corstonian*, a magazine Terry compiled and published, and he would send back pages of handwritten praise. His admiration and respect were so genuine and so generous that he rang me to ask me to collect as many references as possible so he could apply for an honour from Buckingham Palace for Terry. I didn't need to plead or try to canvass support for this, and the response was humbling and exciting. Villagers, the rector and even the ex-head of educational welfare from Avon House all sent evidence of Terry's outstanding contribution to village life. I sent it all off to Sid through the post, and to our surprise and delight a letter arrived, dated 3 May 2006, from Downing Street. It said:

> The Prime Minister has asked me to inform you, in strict confidence that he has in mind, on the occasion of the forthcoming list of Birthday Honours, to submit to the

Queen with a recommendation that her Majesty may be graciously pleased to approve that you may be appointed a Member of the Order of the British Empire (M.B.E.).

That was one hell of a day. We jumped for joy, but were forbidden to tell anyone, not even close family, so we had to curtail an impulse to shout from the rooftops. But the moment the Birthday Honours were published we got going with loud jubilation. We so wanted our entire family of children to attend Buckingham Palace as their father was honoured, but we were allowed only three visitors to accompany Terry so we had to select with care. I would go with Terry, and his oldest son would make up our party. Andrew lived and worked in London, so he was able to help a great deal. We couldn't ask any other of our remaining children to make up a trio to accompany Terry. It would have been too difficult and divisive; so we were just three, with Andrew representing all the children, and it was three expensive outfits and hats I bought before I decided on the one I would wear for Buckingham Palace.

What excitement! We were buzzing, but anxious in case we would somehow derail the proceedings because we were so ignorant of protocol.

Terry wore his hired royal suit and top hat, and on 12 December 2006 we set off by taxi from the London Elizabeth Hotel at Hyde Park. Terry was taken to a separate area for the recipients of awards, and Andrew and I had nominated seats with a wonderful view of the staging in the Great Hall. Music was playing in the Minstrels' Gallery and all was well. I was a tiny shuddering bit anxious because Terry said he would walk without a stick when he approached the Queen. Troubling for me because he often stumbled and frequently fell awkwardly, even when using his trusted stick.

The line-up of recipients walked across the back of the great hall to the holding room, where they would be called individually and announced before they received their medals.

Mozart, Handel and Schubert were played as the award winners paraded across the back of the hall. Then in marched Terry, without his stick, head held high and smiling. The music changed at Terry's entrance. Instead of quiet, sober music they played the romping tune of 'The King Is in His Altogether'. My musical husband responded and stepped out in style. Andrew and I giggled, but we were proud observers of our man, who brought dignity when there could have been mirth.

Buckingham Palace was decorated for Christmas and was awesomely impressive, decorated and festooned with greenery along the stairways. There were elaborate flower arrangements in every space along with a huge Christmas tree in the main foyer. Breathtakingly beautiful and totally impressive.

Andrew took us to lunch at one of his favourite restaurants, and his wife Christina joined us before she picked the children up from school.

A glorious and wonderful occasion and a day full of pride for all Terry had accomplished.

On our return the whole village turned out for an MBE celebration in the village hall and I read the poem I had written to remind everyone of the journey Terry had made from his evacuee days. What a brave spirit!

For Terry – The Love of My Life

A long time ago when armies were marching us all into war
A ten-year-old Terry such bombings he saw.
Planes they were coming from over the sea.
Such was the horror in London city
That the parents of Terry, who worried and fretted,
They sent him away to be evacuated.

Near Appleby town, so far from his home,
In Westmorland county he was left on his own.
Long lonely years in the Lake District spent –
That was the place where our Terry was sent.

This young boy, uncared for, he dared to survive;
Quite independent, he managed to thrive.
Off to catch rabbits, the hills he explored –
He was quite a wild creature. His spirit it soared.

Such a character is Terry, so strong and so brave –
He just keeps on going when others would cave.
This fighting spirit has burned in his heart
All through the years, when we were apart.

Minesweepers, teacher training and then on to teach –
The wheel kept on turning – nothing out of his reach.
Such strength he displayed as one of those cogs
Such skills he could use – on the Island of Dogs.
Then Terry was married, soon after the war –
His first wife was Hilda, five children she bore.
But life was not good for Terry, our man –
Life does not suit us when sh— hits the fan.
So off he did go in his small caravan.

Away went our Terry, he drove far and wide,
He searched for his Julie to be by his side.
But Julie was struggling at the ends of the earth,
But returned here to England, the place of her birth.

A very sad person I was in those days,
But we searched for each other in so many ways.
He found me and saved me and kept me from harm –
He rescued my spirit at a farm called Birk's Barn.

Two children I had then, so pure and so good –
He's been loving towards them, they've been understood.
So, together we faced life and tried to be strong.
Now Terry's been honoured for all that he's done.
To London we've been, spruced up and really serene.
"You've done well and achieved much, good man," said the
Queen.

How lucky we are! What good fortune we've had
When Terry chose Corston, and that can't be bad!
A house in a village that's really a treat –
Such good people here, we are so glad to meet.

So five children had he – I had two of my own –
And then we had Sarah; now the nest she has flown.
A baby to share and give it our love,
We are certain this bundle was sent from above.

He became a head teacher and then he retired;
He's worked for this village even when he was tired.
A talented muscian, his music brings cheers,
But we have to admit that he likes a few beers!

Dedication to the village, so much he has given.
Corstonian produced – to this he was driven.
This corner of England, together we stand –
Thank you, dear villagers. You're really quite grand.

So here in our Corston on each other we lean.
Eight children we have, grandchildren nineteen.
Our life is perfection – what more could we need?
Good friends and relations and now MBE'd!

CHAPTER 41

OVERTURE TO A VERY NASTY WASP STING

The suspicion that something was amiss in the thinking capacity of my wonderful and talented husband crept insidiously into my consciousness. Little signs began to nudge me into an acceptance that all was not as well as it should be in Terry's mind.

He gave ten pence to the window cleaner instead of £10 and insisted it was enough. He couldn't remember the type of beer he normally ordered in the pub. He constantly lost his possessions, such as car keys and glasses; even his false teeth he failed to locate one morning. I found them in his shoes. He kept, annoyingly, sending the television on to a blank or flickering screen and I had to Tippex a line around the volume indicators in order to guide him. Gradually he became incapable of switching on the central heating, answering the phone or using his computer. A kind neighbour would try and correct his mistakes, but in the end the frustration was too much for both of us and we gave the computer away. I had been of no use as I am computer-illiterate and have an aversion and a distrust of all things technical. I have never switched on a computer in my life or sent an email – not even a text message – so I was simply useless in helping to correct my husband's technological chaos. Children would veer away from me in computer rooms at school. Some were so distrustful of me that they would shake their heads in horror as I drew near and make the sign of the cross.

A faithful member of the office staff, Elsie, took pity on me and took over all the technology needed for my work – programmes, timetables, official letters and even photocopying she took on board and without complaint. I will love her forever.

My work in school satisfied me right to the edges of my existence. I seemed to have won the battle for what I believed to be the right approach to survival-English teaching. I had grown to believe implicitly that my work towards the true survival of these needy children was not simply finding a format for teaching the English language speedily, but for endeavouring to sustain them emotionally and spiritually. I had begun to realise that I had the capacity to relieve pain and anguish and replace the torment an individual might be experiencing, with joy, purpose and hope. Was I creating rainbows for these brave young people?

But the torment in my home life was worsening by the minute.

In 2008 we holidayed in Whitby. We had moments when we could enjoy the Beijing Olympics together, then he would disappear into his own mind once again and I couldn't reach him. On our return we had promised our daughter Sarah that we would drive to the caravan site near Weymouth where she was on holiday with her husband and three boys and expecting her fourth baby. What a nightmare journey! Terry drove through all the tiny narrow one-way streets full of pedestrians. I thought we would never leave that maze of tiny streets.

Sarah said, "When you get home I don't want you being driven by Dad again. He is so dangerous and not in control of that big car." She even wrote to the DVLA to stop her dad driving, but the doctor tested his eyesight and blood pressure (but not his reflexes or judgements) so he was pronounced safe to drive.

Neighbours were telling me that Terry shouldn't be driving, but he was still desperate to get to the pub at lunchtimes. On one occasion a villager came to the door to tell Terry that he hadn't used his handbrake. I went outside and found two old ladies stopping the car from rolling down the hill. Even then he continued to drive the car up to his local pub, until two accidents stopped him for good. For a time a good friend picked him up and taxied him to the pub, until Terry's instability made it so difficult and so stressful for his drinking pals that he became virtually housebound.

It had always been my dream to spend a holiday in a castle. Moats and four-poster beds and tapestries featured in the romantic picture I had in mind. We booked a week in a castle ten miles from Edinburgh. We paid £740 for the return trip on the train, first class. Was this the last holiday we would have?

Bad start. Just as the train pulled into Temple Meads to take us to Edinburgh Terry disappeared. I shouted for him and left all the luggage on the platform in order to make a hurried and desperate hunt for my husband.

I was shouting, "He has dementia. Don't let our train go!" And I think I was crying.

He came sauntering down a private staircase; he had gone to find a toilet. I had to quickly find him his seat, then, in a panic, return for all our bags and suitcases. I thought my heart would burst through my ribcage. I knew he couldn't help it, but I was so angry with him that I very nearly punched him.

As if that wasn't enough trauma for one day, he

did exactly the same thing on arrival at Edinburgh. He disappeared from the taxi rank, and I had to ask a stranger to look after the cases whilst I went in search of my husband.

We arrived safely at the castle and were immediately shocked by the number of stairs we had to climb after being assured that the whole of this twelfth-century building had been extensively modified for guests with disabilities.

I was extremely stressed and very tired. I had been looking forward to a five-star meal in their Dungeon Restaurant in the evening and had bought an elegant outfit for this occasion. I couldn't be bothered to change out of my travelling clothes, so we just set off for a pre-dinner drink in the Library Bar up many, many more stone steps. I had to hold Terry from the back going upwards and in front coming downwards because he fell so easily and was constantly banging his poor head. I felt lonely and utterly desperate.

Terry had a beer and I had a juice drink. I had long abstained from any alcohol as it not only affected my blood pressure, but I had seen the diminished lives caused by the abusive intake of the stuff.

We managed to reach the Dungeon Restaurant, which was pristine clean in an unfriendly way, and standing sentry around us were suits of armour and all the relics of medieval warfare.

On each of the dining tables, which were adorned with the most beautiful and fine Irish linen tablecloths and napkins, was an elegant and lit candle. We ordered consommé, which barely covered the base of the soup dish, and we opened up our napkins. Then Terry, to my amazement, produced the most bizarre behaviour that I could ever have imagined. He opened up his napkin, smoothed it out with his hands, then carefully placed it over the lit candle. It rose like a hot-air balloon for a second or two then burst into foul-smelling flames. I grabbed it and bashed it between my hands and pushed the smouldering embers into my handbag.

Moments later the head waiter (or perhaps she was the manager) rushed into the restaurant and said in a strong Scottish accent, "Where's the fire? Where's the fire?" I was totally embarrassed and totally disconcerted.

In an effort to calm her down I said in as calm a voice as I could muster, "It's OK, I've dealt with it. It was an accident."

She said, "But where *is* the fire?" Now she was clearly upset and angry.

I opened my handbag, but the napkin, to my horror, was still alight, burning merrily alongside my purse and handbag contents. She rushed off, only to return with a bucket of water, and I deposited the lit napkin in the water. Terry went on eating his soup, quite unperturbed.

We had to pay for the rest of the meal, which we had ordered but not eaten. We climbed the stone steps back to the Library Bar. I felt I needed a brandy, which would be the first alcohol I had tasted in over twelve years, and I asked Terry what he wanted. The barman stood waiting. Terry didn't know what he wanted.

Then the barman started tapping his foot impatiently, so I just said, "One large brandy, please."

When he returned with the drink I gave it to Terry, who took a sip and shivered.

I thought, 'What the hell am I putting this poor man through? This is no holiday for him.' A few years earlier he would have been stomping out tunes on the piano and everyone would have been singing, but instead everyone was staring.

I looked at Terry and said, "Do you want to go home?"

The look of relief on his face was immediate. He nodded and said in his now very slow drawling voice, "Can you fix it, Julie?"

I sat Terry in our room and begged him to stay put. I went down to reception to say we had to leave first thing in the morning and that my husband couldn't manage. Would they book us a taxi to take us to the railway station? We wouldn't require breakfast. Instead I asked if we could have tea and biscuits at 7.30 a.m. in our room and then we would leave for home.

I helped Terry to dress in the morning. I showered, but put on the same clothes. I couldn't bear to open the cases. A young porter arrived to take us down. The management were clearly glad to see us go. They even returned some of the money we had paid as a deposit on the holiday.

A different young porter came to help us load up the taxi, and he must have heard about us. I managed to laugh out loud when he looked at me and said in an even stronger accent than the head waiter's, "Och, you're the lady with a wee fire in her handbag."

We had one night in a castle, but as we reached home it was the most beautiful, comfortable and safe sight imaginable.

Home – what a wonderful word!

CHAPTER 42

A BRIEF RESPITE AS SOMEONE GIVES ME MY SOUL BACK

At the school where I worked was a female deputy head who really seemed to admire the way I worked. She was called Eileen and she commanded respect from each and every member of staff.

We came to the realisation that we were receiving on to the school roll not only young people needing to learn English, but those who were also deeply troubled.

Many of these were Somalis, Syrians, Congolese and Afghans; and now there were dozens of Polish students.

Together with Eileen and Theresa Thorne, the head teacher, we set up a 'Survival Strategy'. This we hoped would incorporate not just an English language programme, but also a way of relieving pain, stress, loss, isolation, bewilderment and sometimes anger. When Eileen left the school she wrote me a letter which I will treasure forever. She will always be my rainbow and I will treasure her words into eternity. She wrote:

My dearest Julie,

Who could have known, all those years ago when you sat in my office in a school that was falling down, what an important person you would become in my life. From the moment that I saw you with our vulnerable and special children, I knew that you had been sent for a purpose. You have nurtured and cared for our students and given them the gift of a voice. More than this though, you have raised their self-esteem and held their spirits in your hand until they were strong enough to carry them themselves.

You are one of life's special people Julie. Your support for the work that I have tried to do has been immense. You have been like a guardian angel to me. Not the traditional image of an angel I grant you! Your lovely wicked sense of humour, your genuine empathy and understanding and your strong North Country pragmatism have carried me through many a hard day.

Your 'cupboard' has been an oasis of calm and a place that I see all manner of people heading for when they need a little space and love. I am proud to include myself in that number. You never ask why people are interrupting you. You just welcome them in and let them walk out later minus their cares!

I will truly miss you Julie. Thank you for everything.

Lots of love,

Eileen.

I feel so lucky that I met such wonderful people. Elsie, who worked in the office, had single-handedly saved me from a great deal of embarrassment; and we both knew that in today's teacher employment market I wouldn't stand a chance without the ability to transmit data electronically, however skilled a teacher I might happen to be. My aversion is built on a real fear that I would, against my knowledge or will, be drawn into a virtual world – one which I would not be able to escape.

To be able to read distress in another's demeanour is totally dependent on their physical presence.

This belief was reinforced one day as I was on break-time duty and huge crowds of children were frenziedly rushing towards one space near the tennis courts. They were unstoppable and all shouting, "Fight, fight, fight."

It was a stampede! I rushed into school to get help, knowing the situation was dangerous and that I was unable to cope alone.

In each office was a member of staff working on a computer screen. I thought then, perhaps it's better to be listening to a pupil face-to-face rather than perusing data that has already been written or data to do with the planning of the future. We must be in tune with the moment and listen to what is brewing. I can see clearly the benefits of instant information gathering and distribution, but it isn't the answer to all the world's problems. Having said that, I feel the necessity to make my observation that to note what has happened and what could or should happen is important, but observing what is happening at the moment is crucial.

CHAPTER 43

THE BEGINNING OF DEMENTIA

Terry's state of mind continued to worsen. The decline seemed to arrive in lumps and bumps. He now couldn't remain on his own. If I disappeared for longer than he anticipated he would dial 999. His declining memory remembered that number. Coming back from shopping one day he reached for the first bag of shopping, which I'd left at the door. When I'd gone back to the car for the other bags, he tried to assist me by bringing the shopping into the house. He reached down, lost his balance and fell head first into the garden. Sadly his forehead landed hard on a tin of soup. What an injury! Blood everywhere. I heaved him to his feet and sat him at the kitchen table. The phone in the kitchen wasn't working, so I left him so I could ring 999 from the front lounge.

My neighbour arrived to assist, and for over ten minutes we tried to stem the blood using all my tea towels. I rang 999 again and this time the ambulance arrived within a few minutes.

"Thank you," I said to the efficient and kindly ambulance men.

One of them said, "We had to come quickly – we knew it was serious because you called us 'bleeding w------'!"

I was frantically worried about Terry, but his expression didn't change. He was smiling sweetly and clearly didn't realise how very seriously he had been injured. He needed seventeen stitches. It was slow to heal because the cut had not only dented his poor head, but was exactly on old scar tissue. He had hurt the exact same spot twice previously – once falling over a plant pot as he came out of the pub late at night and once again falling from a stepladder as he was fixing the loft hatch on the landing at the top of the stairs.

This last head injury seemed to accelerate his decline, and our doctor in the nearby village of Saltford was constantly trying to help me with the care of my husband. Terry had appointments at the Falls Clinic in Bath. The mental-health agency based at Midsomer Norton had also helped me to obtain a carer's allowance, which I used to pay a private carer in order for me to get to work two or three days a week. Terry refused to attend day-care centres and was adamant that he could manage alone even if I went to work. He had to be humoured and cajoled into accepting another person in the house to watch over him.

The surprising aspect of my husband's heartbreaking decline was that the sadder my heart became, the more I was able to lose myself in my work in school. It was an escape, a relief and a sanctuary where I was able to concentrate and truly be myself and almost forget the disintegration of my home life.

The decline was deepening and it was harrowing for the family. I would soften the edges of my despair as I watched him becoming less and less of the man I adored and had so joyously married forty years before. I would stabilise my emotions then jump as I was thrown into yet another downward leap and I found I was observing full-blown dementia.

On one visit to the hospital we were being interviewed again by yet another specialist who was trying to stem Terry's tendency to constantly fall. He asked me for the earliest indication or sign of Terry's decline. I told him that sixteen years earlier, after playing the organ in church for evensong, Terry had said to me, "I can't play the organ any more because I can't feel my feet on the pedals."

The specialist said, "That's Parkinson's disease."

That was the reason he was constantly falling.

I so wanted to help my darling husband. My heart ached and ached. 'Perhaps I should give up work,' I thought. I had retired twice before – once at sixty years of age and again at sixty-four – but had been invited back because of a fresh intake of refugees and asylum seekers. Also, I really loved my job and felt I was actually helping to mend a troubled world. My work fed my spirit and nourished my capacity to reach troubled young people. Had I to give my work up completely?

CHAPTER 44

THE FIERCELY WASPISH WASPS

I kept wondering how much longer I could go on watching over my beloved Terry. How could I manage to be responsible for what remained of him?

One day, bringing washing down from upstairs in my blue washing basket, I misjudged the bottom two steps and fell heavily on my already damaged knees from a previous accident. Once I'd fallen on a metal rounders base in a school storeroom, and then in Bristol I was waiting in a space to cross a one-way street when a car reversed into my already weakened right knee.

This time I couldn't get up. To my horror Terry had heard the crash, came to look, stared and then calmly ignored my distress, walked back to his easy chair and went on watching the television. I dragged myself to the banister rail and, after several attempts, managed to struggle to my feet. The realisation that Terry could no longer register or recognise the pain in others eclipsed my mind for many weeks after this incident, and some days I felt so sorry for myself I just sat and sobbed. This also prompted no reaction in him whatsoever.

The very, very worst episode was yet to come, and it caused me to wonder even more about my capability to handle the dreadfulness of caring for a body which contained no functioning mind.

It had become routine to get Terry out of bed, washed, hair combed, teeth cleaned, and face the horribleness of getting socks on to uncooperative feet, helping him to dress and bringing him downstairs for breakfast. Then I would give him a Weetabix with milk and sugar, a piece of toast and marmalade and a cup of tea and he would gaze at the newspaper which a kind neighbour brought for us, but not read it or turn the pages, and then I would take him back upstairs and sit him on the toilet and clean him up afterwards. But this particular day in late August 2012 he had an appointment for a blood test at the local surgery in Saltford at 10.45 a.m. – not a good time for my Terry.

I drove him to the surgery and sat in the waiting room awaiting Terry's return from the nurse who was administering the test.

He duly arrived safely back into my care, but I needed to get milk from the Tesco outlet next to the pharmacy which adjoined the doctor's surgery. There was a queue, so rather than make Terry endure queuing I sat him in the car to wait for me to drive him home.

As I came out with my carrier bag full of cartons of milk, I saw to my horror that he was no longer in the car. I could also see an elderly woman pointing at a pile of poo and a pharmacy assistant in a white coat endeavouring to calm the woman down. She was armed with a huge roll of kitchen paper.

I put my hands together in prayer and said, "Please, God, let it be dog sh——." Then I spotted a trail of the poo leading to the door of the doctor's surgery.

With trembling legs I followed the trail of excrement. I was still praying. I opened the door into the surgery waiting room and was greeted by the most appalling smell. Piles of human excrement were dotted across the carpeted waiting area and uncomfortable people with unbelieving eyes and mouths pursed up, apparently holding their breath, were seated around the waiting room. I followed the trail of poo down the carpeted ramp and along a corridor leading to the toilet facility.

I called out, "Are you OK, Terry?"

"Yes, fine" was his reassuring answer. "I'll be out in a minute."

The smell hit me as he opened the toilet door and I led him to the car through the waiting room, where the receptionists were busy with yet more kitchen paper and disinfectant sprays. In a fashion reminiscent of a royal nod, my head swished from side to side as I apologetically walked my husband through the waiting room full of disbelieving people innocently awaiting their doctor's appointments.

I sat Terry in my little car and drove the mile home with my head out of the car window gasping for fresh air. Once home, I stood Terry by the kitchen sink and removed all of his clothing. Poo everywhere, even squashed up his armpits. He surely hadn't eaten enough to provide this amount of poo; he must have been storing it for weeks.

I gingerly took out Terry's purse, his comb and his glasses case from his trouser pockets and put all his clothes – except for shoes, which I washed and put on the garden seat outside to dry – into a big black bin liner.

Terry stood stark naked whilst I cleaned his poor shivering body and dressed him in clean dry clothes. I then sat him in his favourite chair to watch television whilst I considered what to do next.

To my relief it was Wednesday, our recycling day, and the binmen had not yet picked up our rubbish bags. I put out the bin liner along with our other bags and boxes and, suddenly and surprisingly, felt safer – but not for much longer. This was when I finally lost all composure and restraint and became a volatile dragon of a woman capable of tyrannical abuse of my beloved husband.

I sat close to my husband and held his hand. This gesture had recently become the most reassuring act in dispersing anxiety that I could offer him and had also become a last resort when he needed calming.

Terry looked at me and said, "Wallet."

This is when I became a harridan, an obnoxious, bad-tempered, sarcastic and nasty old woman. I changed from the sweet-natured, positive person people said I was, to a foul creature spitting exasperation and bile on my innocent unsuspecting husband.

"Wallet," he said again. "Depot – ring depot."

Terry's wallet was still in his foul-smelling trousers.

In the minutes between me putting out the sh——-filled trousers and clearing up, the binmen had collected our rubbish.

I said, in a voice I didn't even recognise myself, "Oh, sure, I'll just ring the depot and ask them to look through Corston's bin liners until they find a bin liner full of sh——, find a pair of sh——-filled trousers and look in the pockets until you find a sh——y wallet. Take out his Barclay Card and debit card and send the f------ things back to us. F--- off, Terry, just f--- off!" And then I collapsed in tears of shame and frustration until I was recovered sufficiently to ring the bank and cancel the two cards.

Terry just ignored me and went on watching the television.

Paralysing loneliness ensued.

CHAPTER 45

DEMENTIA HITS OUR LAST HOLIDAY: WASPS GALORE

It was clear to all the family that Terry's mental abilities were fading fast. I could see it every day, but our children, who came regularly but often with monthly gaps between visits, were visibly shocked by his rapid decline.

Our daughter-in-law, who is a senior nurse in a large hospital and renowned for her fearsome composure, was reduced to tears as she observed her father-in-law's struggle to perform the simplest of tasks.

We decided to try one more holiday. I so looked forward to sharing the responsibility for Terry's welfare with more family around.

We booked a huge old rectory in Devon advertised as family-friendly with pets welcome. What a disaster that proved to be!

My daughter Sarah, with her husband, Sean, and her four boys came, plus their dog, Gooby. My eldest daughter, Linda, also came with her daughter Holly. My son, Christopher, would arrive later with his daughter Katy. I was prepared to do all the cooking and shopping, knowing there were other loving members of my treasured family to watch over Terry.

Every single second of that so-called holiday was filled with stress and anxiety. The advertised swimming pool was a small plastic inflatable at the top of a steep incline. The family pet's movements were supposed to be limited to the kitchen, which had windows that did not open; worse still, the downstairs bedroom for Terry had no shower, and the bathroom was two long corridors away. But the worst aspect was Terry's restlessness. I couldn't shut my eyes. When I did try to rest, Terry's hands would hit his chair arms to push himself into a standing position. I couldn't leave him for a second. If I thought he was having a nap, I would creep outside for a moment's fresh air leaving the doors open wide, but it was as if he had an extra sense and I would hear him stumbling about searching for me. If I sat him on the toilet, with Sarah keeping a discreet eye on him through the keyhole, we would all be on tenterhooks anxiously awaiting a crash because he fell so easily.

The worst aspect was trying to sleep at night. I accepted that prostate weakness made him unsure of when he needed a wee, but it began to feel perverse as I struggled to obtain just half an hour's respite from the constant vigilance. I cried tears of frustration throughout the night, knowing the space of time was growing less before I had to wash and dress him ready for the day.

During the first night I pushed my bed against his so I would know if he tried to get out of bed without me because he had fallen in the gap at the other side, hitting his head on the stone surround of an old fireplace. In the early hours I wedged his bed against a flat wall with my bed pushed hard against his, believing if I did nod off he would wake me by trying to climb over me. I felt as if my face was falling off my head with exhaustion. I had no space to see to my own needs. I could feel myself beginning to begrudge the existence of my once wonderful husband. I couldn't enjoy the company of my children or grandchildren. I was completely blocked from everything I had looked forward to so much. Reading stories to my grandchildren, telling them made-up yarns, playing games or just reading my own book or talking to my family was denied me.

But my worst night was to come – a night which made us decide to return home early. I don't know where all the tears came from. I thought there was a limit, but my Sarah heard me from the floor above and came to my rescue. She had her boys to care for – their daily needs of food and clean clothes and the huge demands of watchfulness required in looking after four young boisterous boys was enough for one young mother – but it was her father in a mess and her mother was wailing. How awful for her! Linda was sympathetic, but it was not her father so it was slightly easier to be more objective and detached.

That particular night was utterly awful. I had watched Terry until he fell asleep, then lay down on my bed to try and grab ten minutes' peacefulness. The second I closed my eyes I felt a heavy arm land on my head as Terry flung back his duvet in his attempt to get out of bed. He needed the toilet. I had resorted to using a bucket in our bedroom for him to wee in rather than staggering down two corridors with him to the toilet in a separate wing of the house.

After three goes within twenty minutes I decided that I would put one hair roller on the bookshelf to represent each toilet visit through the night. I had brought my box of pink hair rollers with me from home, but had not yet had the time to wash my hair and use the rollers. By six thirty in the morning I had deposited nineteen rollers on to the bookshelf from my box.

I couldn't do this any more. I was shaking and crying from sheer frustration and anger. Anger, because it felt perverse. I was at his mercy and pleading, "Please rest, Terry, please rest." He couldn't help it, but I knew I was beginning to feel very annoyed with him. Then I was deeply ashamed because I had gripped his arm so tightly as I guided him across the bedroom to the bucket that when I took his pyjama jacket off I could see bruises where my fingers had gripped his arm.

That made me howl like a banshee. I sobbed on his chest saying, "Sorry, Terry. Sorry, my darling. Sorry, my precious man." How could I allow myself to become so frustrated?

Terry just smiled at me and patted my head. I was deeply, deeply ashamed.

The children were having a ball, racing up one staircase and down another with the dog in hot pursuit. Children are wonderful creations. Not for them the anticipated pleasures. Instant gratification is the order of the day. My misery was running alongside absolute joy and freedom of movement.

My son arrived. He had travelled 250 miles to help me. He was going to stay two nights, but he understood that we would go home as soon as we could pack up. Linda had her car and Sarah had her car, but Terry and I had travelled by taxi. Their cars were fully loaded, but Chris had offered to drive Terry and me home and stay overnight with us. Holly had to go back quickly as she was awaiting her GCSE results, and so we set off early on Friday morning, homeward-bound.

I felt as if I'd paid over £2,000 for a living nightmare.

On arriving home, Terry kept asking me to tell him when we were going home. He no longer recognised his own home. Whatever was I to do?

I still feel sad and guilty that I had held Terry's arm too tightly whilst on holiday. My understanding tells me that old people's skin bruises very easily, but even so I was devastated that I had let myself hurt him even a tiny bit during our umpteenth visit to the toilet.

CHAPTER 46

THE EFFECTS OF THE ACCUMULATION OF TOO MANY WASP STINGS

No one can care for another living creature for twenty-four hours a day unless the one cared for settles and sleeps in a dependable fashion for a good chunk of that time.

To be anxious for another's welfare day in and day out is an impossible ordeal. Not to be able to relax enough to enjoy the preparation or the eating of a meal, answer the phone, wash yourself or your hair, visit the toilet or go to the shop, help your children, grandchildren or a neighbour, apply a dab of lipstick, write a thank-you note, read a book or a newspaper or even gaze at your face long enough to remove an offending chin hair is like pressing your self-destruct button.

Life was fast becoming unbearable, and even when I paid a carer to sit with Terry in order to have a moment's respite I was still anxious for his safety and well-being. Every sound made me jump and my skin would tingle as if an electric current had passed through my body. My granddaughter dropped the toilet seat once and I was still shaking half an hour after the bang!

Only in my little job at school did I obtain relief for my jangled nerves. It was only there that I felt like me. School was buzzing with life and exciting exuberance. This made it possible to burst through the boundaries of tension, which was my everyday life at home. Otherwise, in all other circumstances when I couldn't see my husband, I was tense in my mind and my body in a head-spinning kind of way. Had he fallen again or soiled himself? Was he cooperating with the carer? Had he eaten his meal? Had he wandered off and become lost? Was he looking for me?

At the onset of his dementia he had rung the police to tell them I had had an accident when I was only a little later home than he expected. I knew this because when I arrived home the phone rang and it was the police asking if I was Julie Miller and had I had an accident?

As each miserable, fraught day was followed by yet another day filled with tension and heartbreaking mental strain, the realisation was developing that I had lost my beloved husband forever. In his early forgetful days I could canvass for some understanding and some cooperation. I had, in fact, said to our wonderful doctor in the nearby village of Saltford that it was my duty to care for Terry. However, the dementia progressed. Now here I was at my wits' end, crying out for someone to alleviate the strain and rescue me.

I think maybe I could have coped with the memory loss, but not with the falling. If Terry had been less agitated and not so compelled to make sudden decisions to move, I might have managed better, but when he fell he always hit his head. His forehead was now scarred and bumped and his right eyebrow was distorted. I so wanted a good night's sleep – I now fantasised about sitting with a good book and a cup of tea, convinced that that would feel like pure luxury.

My children, grandchildren and stepchildren were unbelievably kind, but they too were now daunted by the simple task of taking Terry for a short walk. Ian, my very thoughtful stepson, volunteered to take his father for a pint at the local pub. When he returned he looked exhausted and told me he wouldn't want to do it again without more family around.

So the day dawned in September 2012 when I couldn't manage another moment without a proper break. For the fifth time in ten minutes I had followed Terry up the stairs to the toilet and preceded him back down again. I was crying. I opened the top of the stable door, which is the front door of our house, and leaned out to obtain a gulp of fresh air. I held on to Terry's clenched fist so I would know where he was. I was actually hyperventilating through choking sobs of self-pity. My beautiful daughter Linda arrived and was clearly shocked at the distress she was witnessing. She didn't leave me until she had got help. She must have phoned all the right agencies because social services, the Mental Health Support group and our doctor worked together to rescue me. My darling daughter had contacted the Carer's Centre, the community health centre, social services and the wonderful, wise and patient coordinator for mental health based at St Martin's Hospital in Bath, Rhys Evans.

Rhys asked to talk to me on the phone. It was hard for him to discern my words because of my distressed sobbing. I was so very tired and very, very guilty that I was now releasing my husband into another's care.

Rhys got the message and said, "I'll find you a place for Terry by tomorrow."

"I can't go through one more night without sleep," I replied.

He rang back. "Get Terry to Charlton House at 7.30 p.m. tonight. They have a room for him there. It's in nearby Keynsham."

Linda knew the place as it backed on to her own home in Keynsham. I had to pack Terry a case and get him some food before we left. This was to be the last time I ever made a meal for my darling, and it was rubbish. Terry liked soft-boiled eggs on toast, but I only had wholemeal bread, which he didn't like. With trembling hands I made him what was to be my final offering of food, and it closely resembled a plate of cat sick!

CHAPTER 47

ALIEN WASPS HARM MY CHILDREN

My first husband, Neil, had always blamed me for the disintegration of his family life. Soon after the divorce he had developed psoriasis, a skin condition which caused red, scaly and itchy patches. According to him I was the cause of this. My son kept in contact with his father, but Linda found her visits to him very difficult. She not only looks very like me, but her attitude to life is very similar. This must have been an irritation to her father, and she often felt defensive regarding his verbal attacks on me, her mother. Her contact with her father became less and less frequent.

Neil's health was failing. His kidneys were not functioning well and he needed dialysis. Again, I was to blame for his poor health, not his greed or his unhealthy lifestyle. Bitterness oozed out of him.

This bitter hatred had been demonstrated in a whole variety of ways. Probably the most hurtful was on the occasion when I asked if he could possibly send me a few colour slides of the transit along the Panama Canal. We were studying great canals at school, and when it was discovered that I had twice travelled that awesome canal I thought, in my innocence or ignorance, that he might send me some slides on the understanding that I would, of course, send them back. I knew he had burned all albums, including our wedding albums, but Christopher had said that he thought his father had kept all the colour slides.

A box of slides marked 'Panama' arrived, much to my delight. The school hall was set up to watch the slide show of Panama. Then the sickening shock came. On each and every slide, where my image could be viewed, my face had been meticulously burned away with what must have been a hot needle. This had been unnoticeable on the tiny slides, but once enlarged on a big screen it was totally visible. This was excruciatingly embarrassing and difficult to explain to a hall full of schoolchildren.

Dialysis had become so painful and so life-limiting for Neil that he was now refusing to undergo the almost daily process.

Neil asked Christopher to visit him on his deathbed. He was now in a hospice in Wolverhampton. Linda decided she would accompany her brother on this final pilgrimage to say goodbye to their dying father.

Christopher was welcomed by his frail father, but the bitterness was still there towards his daughter. Neil asked her why she had come as there was no money for her. Linda is the most unmercenary creature I have ever met, so was deeply hurt by this remark. Then he added, "Your children will never amount to anything. They are useless misfits."

Poor Christopher felt he couldn't challenge his dying father, so he has been left with the guilt. I had to try and mend the horrifying damage this foreign wasp had caused, but I am still endeavouring to mend that hurt and now my Linda was protecting me and driving her stepfather and distressed mother to a care home.

What an ordeal for her!

CHAPTER 48

A BRIEF RESPITE FROM WASP STINGS

Mid September 2012 and we were on our way to Charlton House in Keynsham. I had no knowledge of homes. I did not even understand the difference between a care home and a nursing home, but my precious daughter Linda was driving me to a place that would hopefully give me a chance to recover my peace of mind.

The fragment that remained of my thinking capacity knew how important it was to obtain a moment to myself. Surely when professionals saw my husband's circumstances they would insist on a more permanent residence for him at Charlton House! I had been told by professionals in the world of mental health care that unless other arrangements were made one or both of us would end up hospitalised, so I was hopeful of real help.

We were received at the home with a kind welcome and were shown Terry's room. A tray of tea and biscuits was brought to us and everyone was treating us with respect and dignity. I was asked if I wanted to take Terry's washing to do at home or did I want them to do it? I thought to myself that it was my responsibility and would be the least I could do to help. Of course I would take his washing. Terry had always worn a white shirt and tie, and a clean shirt each day was a part of his life and had been for the past forty years. I could keep that routine going.

I left Terry sitting in the lounge area, seemingly quite unperturbed by his new surroundings. I was concerned that the carers did not know Terry and would not know how driven he was; but I left him there, having first stood watching for five minutes from a safe distance, and felt more relaxed that he remained sitting quietly, innocently gazing around.

Linda and I drove away, arranging to meet later at an Irish/Italian restaurant in Keynsham. For the first time in years I was able to shower and dress in peace.

At eight thirty we ate our wonderful meal. Linda, her two children, Jed and Holly, and I. It was sheer heaven. I ate my favourite scallops with black pudding and felt like punching the air with sheer delight and a new sense of freedom. Linda asked me if I wanted her to stay the night. I so wanted her delicious and comforting presence; but I knew if I couldn't face being alone this night, I wouldn't be able to manage in the future and so I declined her thoughtful offer and went home alone. I kept all my lights on and, for the first time in years, was able to read myself to sleep and then stay asleep right through the night. I felt so much better.

The next day I hurriedly got ready to see my Terry only a few miles away. I had been told I could visit any time and had been given a code to get up to Terry's floor in the lift.

Friday, Saturday, Sunday, Monday – I visited twice a day, just holding his hand, walking around the enclosed garden and drinking lots of tea; but his constant falling was disturbing the general peace of the place, and I was reminded that it was a care home and not a nursing home. Each time I went Terry had fallen again and again. His bumps and bruises were too numerous to count.

Here I was at Charlton House on the Tuesday of that respite week. I had been handed a very large plastic bag containing Terry's clothes full of faeces. All his waste products had been cleaned up from the floor of his en suite and now no one was smiling at me. They were not equipped to deal with people who had no control over their bodily functions. By the time I got to Charlton House on Wednesday I was asked to go to the supervisor's office. They could not keep him there longer than the allocated week's respite. They could not afford the twenty-four-hour care which Terry so urgently needed. They couldn't tell me what to do when the week was up.

I sat with Terry, my poor, poor darling. I held his hand and cried and cried and cried. What was I to do? Who would help me now? Was I to take him home and begin the destructive battle again or simply run away where no one would find me?

CHAPTER 49

A MOMENTOUS LIFE-CHANGING RAINBOW

Never could I have anticipated the desolation I felt thinking I had to take Terry home to restart the agonising routine of round-the-clock care. I knew I couldn't do it – if fourteen professional carers couldn't manage Terry's difficulties, how could I do it alone?

Then my life changed forever. As I sat holding Terry's hand and sobbing loudly, I was told I had a visitor.

In walked Fiona, matron manager of Cholwell House Nursing Home. She sat between us and held on to us.

"Stop crying. I am going to make it possible for you to be Terry's wife again – not just his carer."

From that moment I knew that I had met a remarkable human being who could mend my broken life. Fiona – I will love her forever and ever and ever. She took me into the corridor and the reassurance in her voice and her confidence healed, mended and inspired me. At last I had met someone who truly understood my misery and was going to make better lives for Terry and me. Her delicious Scottish voice resonated with assurance and sympathy. I was no longer alone.

She said, "Tomorrow, a taxi will bring you and Terry to Cholwell House. A carer from Charlton House will accompany you. Pack up his belongings and we'll be waiting for you."

I sobbed even more loudly as my mind took on board her wonderful words. I was rescued. Was God smiling on me? He certainly was.

I can only pray that any carer in a similar position will find a Fiona.

CHAPTER 50

CHOLWELL HOUSE: MY RAINBOW

My walk with Terry up the steps of the nursing home was reminiscent of Alec Guinness's walk from the punishment box in the film *The Bridge on the River Kwai*. A walk totally dependent on willpower and not on the physical ability to move one leg after another.

Would I ever walk out with him again? Would he ever sit in his own leather reclining chair again? Would he ever again show me the very first snowdrop of the new springtime? Would he ever again be able to hold me in his arms and make my world right?

Fiona greeted us like long-lost friends and I realised that the ominous look of the outside of the building was nothing like the inside, where joy, happiness and goodwill was written on all the faces of the carers and nurses. We sat in the conservatory lounge after viewing the room where Terry was to sleep, and at this point I broke down completely and sobbed on Terry's shoulder, gripping his hands until his knuckles turned white. The shock of seeing residents in the last stages of their existence was too much for me. Rocking, dribbling, calling out.

I made a mistake by saying, "I cannot leave my Terry here. He does not fit in here."

Fiona again came to rescue me. She took my hand again and said, "Leave him here tonight and see how you feel tomorrow. He will be cared for every moment of the day and night. Trust us."

I left the building. I stood with the carer from Charlton House, who had stayed with me throughout the introductions at Cholwell House. We waited over half an hour for the taxi to return for us and we talked. My shoulders began to relax – they had been somewhere near my ears. We talked and talked and it was wonderful again to be able to have a conversation without the stress of watching Terry's every move. He was only yards away, but I was tasting freedom once more. The taxi took us back to Charlton House, where I had left my car.

Cholwell House is only eight miles from my home and the drive is through beautiful villages and countryside – and the tension was fading. I could drive again and enjoy trees, clouds, sunshine, deer and rabbits. My soul was beginning to heal and my spirit was mending.

The spirit of Cholwell melted its way into my heart. Fiona had given me back my life. She had changed everything. I was Julie again and was beginning now to learn about how to deal with the wasp stings which had left me bereft, confused, frustrated, lonely and sometimes even angry.

I learned so much and I am still learning. Positive messages can arrive from the most unlikely sources.

The remarkable Fiona was impressing me with her wisdom, professionalism, wit, compassion and her wondrous wickedness. She made me laugh at her naughtiness, which blended painlessly into everyone's attitude to the way we conduct ourselves when dealing with pain and anguish and disturbed minds in others.

To deal day after day with the disintegration of human beings takes stamina, courage and tenacity; it also requires gigantic leaps of faith and, above all, love of humanity (and in Fiona's case this included all living things).

CHAPTER 51

THE CUSHIONING EFFECT OF BRILLIANT CARE AND MANAGEMENT

During the first week of Terry's stay at Cholwell House, I had been somewhat smug. Unlike the other residents Terry could stride about with his trusted stick, visit the toilet practically on his own and eat solid food using a knife and fork. His speech was mostly coherent and he could sit at a dining table for his meals.

On my visits I could go with him to the toilet and hold him upright for him to have a wee; for more prolonged toilet use, I could hold his hand and clean him up when he had finished. He was annoyingly driven to get up and move about constantly, but he would, when seated, point out residents who he thought were crazy.

He also said, "How long do I have to stay here?"

I swallowed hard and said, as reassuringly as possible, "Until you are better, Terry."

This seemed to satisfy him. Then one day, a few weeks after his arrival at Cholwell, I realised to my utmost horror that I was having difficulty preparing him to sit on the toilet. My wonderful, talented, musical and 'put the world right' husband was actually wearing a huge nappy. I made no comment, but in my heart I realised that this was the beginning of a progression towards totally infantile dependence and I had to take it on board. Eventually my Terry would end up bedridden and my visits would be limited to sitting with him in his room with no activity around to break the loneliness and feelings of isolation. This I was dreading.

Soon after, Terry's condition and situation was brought home to me with electrifying clarity.

Fiona asked for a meeting with me. She was being serious and her hallmark of humour was absent. She asked me, "Do you want Terry to be resuscitated if there are no life responses?"

I just said, "I don't want him to suffer. Do not try to bring him back once he's given up."

Fiona wrote this down and I tried to drive home. The reality of our situation was apparent. I had not thought through the demise of my husband, and I was shocked.

I drove home. I realised I was driving quite dangerously, so decided to drive to the Co-operative supermarket at Keynsham, where I could buy myself a latte in their café and try to sort my head out. This supermarket is now the impressive Waitrose, but at that time the café area made good coffee and tuna-melt paninis, which always put me right. I would put five sugars in my coffee – that would help me to feel myself again.

I sat in the café drinking and eating, beginning to feel better and not so shocked, when an announcement came over the Tannoy: "Would the owner of car registration --- --- HH come to reception immediately?"

It was my number! Had someone bashed into my car? No – in my shocked state I hadn't put my handbrake on and my car had run into a posh car and then stopped when it could run no further. My brain went into overdrive and I had to really struggle to sort out the mess without losing my no-claims bonus on my car insurance.

How do I prepare myself for the loss of my husband?

Have I said goodbye already?

What is a body without a mind?

Where do I seek comfort?

Have I used up all my emotional energy and resources?

Is there some God-given courage that might be hiding inside me, and will it emerge when I can no longer visit him and hold his hand?

How will I cope without the man who made me feel beautiful and needed?

How will I manage without the husband who provided me with the baby I so wanted?

How did we manage to love each other's children as well as our own?

Would my strength of character re-emerge?

Perhaps I can help other carers who are feeling the same, going through a similar ordeal. I must not depend on my children and grandchildren to give my life purpose and meaning. They have their lives to live.

I must not become a burden.

All these things were going through my mind as I sorted out the damage to another person's precious vehicle, and I thought, 'At the moment Terry is still alive at Cholwell House.'

I drove straight back there and held his hand once more – much to the surprise of the carers.

"Back again?" they all said.

CHAPTER 52

THE INSPIRATION I FOUND AT CHOLWELL HOUSE AND THE WASP STINGS ARE FADING

As I became more and more familiar with the regime of care at this outstanding home, I began to realise, without a fraction of a doubt, that the amazing standard of care sprang from its leader, Fiona. Each and every member of staff was trained in her schedule of finding that fragment of humanity which remains in every human being until we take our last breath and nourishing it in ways I previously never thought possible.

This routine of care and nourishment seemed almost to be a form of subliminal advertising. Reassurances were handed out with such constancy it was overwhelming to observe.

No resident was ignored as the carers and nurses, administration staff and helpers went about their business. A touch, a word, a cuddle or a kiss were constant reminders that each resident was important. *Subliminal* because often the recipient of this delightful routine was half asleep or even loudly swearing at another nearby resident, or even kicking out.

As I watched these messages of goodwill from the staff as they passed each and every resident, regardless of the behaviour they presented to the world, I became more and more humbled as I realised my own tolerance had fallen far short of that of these gracious and patient carers. I was humbled – even more so because the grace and goodwill was also directed at me. I was greeted, on each of my visits, with hugs and shouts of delight as I came through the door. What heart-lifting joy they bestowed on all who entered the doors of Cholwell! And I not only grew dependent, but actually looked forward to seeing their dear faces. There was always a hot drink awaiting all visitors and the feeling of being cherished was beginning to dispel all memory of the many wasp stings I had endured before our arrival at this magical place.

I tried to see Terry every day, including the days I worked in school, but driving from Fishponds, Bristol, to Temple Cloud on those working days proved too much. I was having nosebleeds – something I had never experienced in my life before. The care and consideration which reached the visitors as well at the residents at this home became evident to me when on arrival there after an exhausting day at school, followed by a long drive in heavy traffic, I was told I looked pale and wan.

Becky, a nurse, said, "I want to take your blood pressure."

I resisted, but she insisted, looking quite concerned about my health. My blood pressure had sky-rocketed and I was sent home immediately.

Becky told me to see the doctor or, at least, stop lashing myself. " You must look after yourself – your husband needs you. Don't drive yourself into the ground."

I haven't been to a doctor for almost forty years except with Terry. I had always been adamant and totally convinced that a human body has the infinite capacity to heal itself if you give it the right help, so I decided to sort out my visiting times in a more user-friendly fashion. I would visit Terry on Wednesdays, Fridays, Saturdays and Sundays, leaving Mondays and Tuesdays for my school days; and I would call Thursdays my 'Julie days', when I would relax, have my lunch in a nice café, clean up at home and try not to feel guilty.

I felt so much better in this more comfortable routine, and my visits to Terry became more special. My blood pressure subsided and my nosebleeds stopped completely.

I must mention one very special lady who came to visit regularly and was so very supportive. This was the representative nurse from the Continuing Health Care department of the NHS.

Her name was Karen and it was as if all the world's calmness had been deposited in one person. She understood everything about the carers of dementia patients. The guilt, the self-doubt and the pain you endure in seeing your loved one looking the same but now completely different. My darling husband was in the same body, but was a different man. All this Karen demonstrably understood, and her effect on my well-being was dramatic. I hope all other carers of dementia sufferers have the good fortune to meet such people who are positive and life-affirming and who cleverly push the demons away.

I also had the greatest of blessings in meeting Sharon, who is a carer and art-and-craft specialist at Cholwell House. Never in my life have I met a more life-affirming and positive human being. She sees the fun in every aspect of human difficulty and endeavour. She has made me laugh when I know, without her, I would have been in tears. I am very, very lucky that she is in my life and she says that she always will be.

God bless her for the sheer wickedness of her humour.

CHAPTER 53

THE PROGRESSION OF DEMENTIA

Over the period of time that Terry lived his life at Cholwell I began to observe a sequence which showed the gradual disintegration of a human being whose life was blighted by dementia. To me there is an observable progression of diminishing abilities which occurs in the decline of dementia sufferers. These are the stages which I detected:

- Simple forgetfulness.
- Worsening and life-affecting forgetfulness.
- Growing dependence on others.
- Deepening dependence on others and requiring twenty-four-hour care and provision of everyday needs.
- Carer can cope no longer.
- Doctor's assessment.
- Mental-health agencies' assessment and intervention.
- Social-services' intervention.
- Attendance or carer's allowance no longer sufficient incentive against the destructive forces of dementia.
- Frequently, perhaps invariably, other health issues affect the decline of a dementia sufferer:

1. Prostate problems in men.
2. Inactivity affecting legs and causing problems with circulation.
3. Sight and hearing loss.
4. Anxiety issues.
5. Coordination and disorientation issues causing frequent falls.
- The sufferer shows complete lack of appreciation for another's comfort or peace of mind.
- Once safely established in a nursing home, the suferer's routines disintegrate into fragments as capabilities decrease.
   1. Eats with knife and fork at a dining table after choosing food from menu.
   2. Eats with fork only when food has been cut in manageable pieces.
   3. Stays in lounge chair and eats meal from movable tray/table.
   4. Eats with spoon only.
   5. Food minced to soft pulp.
   6. Fed by carer using spoon.
   7. Spends long periods of time asleep.
   8. Dribbles from nose and mouth, requiring constant attention from carers.
   9. Moved with hoist.
   10. Unable to cooperate in movement or toilet visits.
   11. Twenty-four-hour use of nappies.
   12. Bedridden. Simply sleeping, fed, changed and staring. Sometimes calling for help, mother or home.

This was the stage I dreaded, cut off from the everyday activity of the nursing home, and this is where I was. I had to face it. The progression of this terrible ailment had left me visiting a man who closely resembled my beloved husband, but now there was nothing to remind me of the life we had together. I even missed the rows we used to have. Two people battling it out to see who would end up victorious. Me bursting into tears would often mean that Terry would relent and let me have my own way.

But the people who worked in the nursing home saved the day. The care and support I so desperately needed was there in those people, who gave their life energy to the care of vulnerable people. Their generous care disempowered the relentless progression of wasp stings and they made rainbows for me.

CHAPTER 54

WASP STINGS CAUSED THROUGH REFLECTION

During Terry's stay at Cholwell House I would often be stopped in my tracks by my thoughts. Mostly I would write them down, because putting words on paper helped me to organise my thinking and usually stopped me from falling into a distressed and incoherent place.

5 January 2014

I have just dismantled my Christmas tree. I am overcome with sadness. Instead of life becoming easier, with me becoming more accustomed to living alone, I feel more desolate than I have ever felt and further away from my life-sharing mate. Now I am thinking that this is the second springtime, about to arrive, when my Terry will not take my hand and show me the first snowdrops of the year which he has just spotted. He never will again and I have to face it.

I am trying to be positive – really, really trying, but sadness sweeps over me unhindered by any hopes for a wonderful, happy future. I will read my Sarah's poem again and perhaps Eileen's letter too.

This is Sarah's poem, written for me for Mother's Day 2007.

I feel so very lucky to have a mum like you
You are reflected in my life in everything I do
When I face a challenge, problem or any kind of choice
I think of what you would do, I hear your gentle voice.

You've loved me and cared for me and taught me how to be
A person who is thoughtful and appreciate all I see
You protect me and help me all of the time
You've made me so strong that a mountain I could climb.

My friends are so envious of me they want you for their mum
So when I tell them things you do they end up feeling glum.
What would I be without you? I'd be sensible and boring
Instead, I love the world and life is all enthralling.

You are a mum like no other, a shining twinkling star
Shining brighter than the others and the prettiest by far
So thank you Mum for being you and teaching me so well
You are so wise and wonderful and absolutely swell.

I love you.
Lots and lots of love from Sarah.

Valentine's Day 2014

I remember when I gave a talk at Bishopston Teachers Centre in Bristol on Valentine's Day 1984. As I delivered my little speech the door opened and one of the workers, half hidden by a huge bunch of red roses, entered the room and handed me the roses. The attached note read, 'Julie, I love you, from Terry.'

Now, thirty years later, there are no roses or messages of love. I am, once again, bereft. Life experiences have taught me much and I can use those lessons as a bridge between what I had and what I have now. I must use those lessons as a means of nurturing positive feelings in myself and all whom I meet in schools, in nursing homes, in my village and in all my dealings in everyday life. This takes me to a good place and I must allow myself space to be steered along life's paths. I just have to listen.

20 February 2014

I am listening hard to the world around me. At the moment my work with children arriving from far-off and dangerous places sustains me. At the same time visiting my husband, feeding him small pieces of nectarine or knitting him colourful waistcoats also fills me with happiness and purpose. The people who work at Cholwell House fill the leftover spaces with joy. Yesterday I arrived to find our wonderful life-affirming Sharon dressed as Little Bo-Peep, complete with shepherd's crook. She was surrounded by smiling residents. Dan was dressed as a Mexican bandit with poncho and sombrero as part of his outfit. Becky was dressed up in a Mary Poppins outfit and moved from resident to resident spreading light and laughter. There seemed no connection with the choices of apparel, but it was infectiously hilarious.

CHAPTER 55

RELENTLESS, DEADLY WASP STINGS DISEMPOWERED BY LOVE AND CARE

By May this year, 2014, Terry was clearly deteriorating at a rate of knots. His decline was escalating and he wasn't eating or drinking as he normally did. I had handed my notice in at school in order to spend more time at Terry's bedside. He was lying in bed, with the nurse coming in to turn him from time to time and give him a small amount of liquid from a spoon. This he had difficulty swallowing, and the liquid mostly dribbled back out of his mouth.

My brother and sister-in-law came down from Yorkshire along with my sister-in-law's sister, Christine, who had arrived from America, where she has lived for the past fifty or more years.

On 16 May Michael and I went to see Terry at Cholwell House. The two sisters went into Bath to see the sights of that Georgian city. My brother was clearly distressed to see Terry looking so very ill and unable to recognise anyone. We returned home and Michael said, "You must have a day off tomorrow. We will give you a happy day. Where would you like to go?"

My reply was "The American Museum, please. They have an art and textile knitting exhibition on at the moment and they serve wonderful lunches. That would be really good."

The four of us had a wonderful time. The sun shone and the exhibition was glorious. It was Kaffe Fassett knitting on display and I was in my element. I had such a happy day.

My family were due to return to Yorkshire the next day, which was Sunday 18 May. They were just about to set off home when the phone rang. It was Fiona from Cholwell House. Terry was not responding at all. I waved my worried family off and set off to the nursing home. My brother would have stayed and supported me, but he had to get Christine back to pack up for her return flight to America.

I drove the eight miles to Cholwell with my heart spasmodically exploding in my chest and my head pounding. I was quickly shown to Terry's room, where I found him barely alive. The nurses were quiet and sympathetic and – unusually – unsmiling.

They were reassuring when I asked how long I had left with Terry. "Could be today or could be tomorrow, but he is in no pain."

I stroked his thin body very gently. He had just a thin sheet covering him. I was shocked to find him so thin that what I thought was his heel on his bent leg was actually his hip bone. I was given a pot containing oily sticky liquid and what looked like a large baby cotton bud, which I was to dip in the slimy liquid and moisten his dry mouth and lips.

Unknown to me, Fiona had phoned Terry's second daughter, Alison, who had been a frequent visitor to Cholwell, and told her that her father was not long for this world. Sadly she was in bed and was shockingly ill with a serious stomach upset, but she had sent her wonderful husband, Nick. Alison was devastated that she was unable to come; but even if she had dragged herself from her sickbed, no one would have allowed her in. The norovirus had struck Cholwell the first Christmas Terry was in residence there and it was quarantined for six weeks, when no visitors were allowed to visit their loved ones.

Our youngest daughter, Sarah – the child who belonged to both Terry and me – had also been alerted, but she had to sort out her large family of boys and travel the thirty miles from Gillingham in Dorset. I was told she wanted to get to me as quickly as possible. But in walked our son-in-law Nick. The whole family regarded him as a superhero. He is magnificent with his large handlebar moustache and strong physique. He has trained military personnel in Iraq, Afghanistan and Ireland and received the MBE for his work organising the dignified reception of the fallen soldiers from those volatile and dangerous areas of our world, and here he was making me feel a whole lot safer.

I kept saying to him, "Don't stay too long, because your poorly wife needs you," but I really didn't want him to leave me alone.

His reply was "I will stay until Sarah arrives, and she's on her way."

There we stayed, occasionally moistening Terry's lips and inside his mouth and us drinking copious amounts of tea. Sandwiches arrived at lunchtime and large pieces of cake from the wonderful carers. At two o'clock Sarah arrived with her son Joshua, our thirteen-year-old grandson. He is the most articulate of Sarah's four boys and I was pleased to see him, if not a little alarmed that he might not cope with witnessing the final moments of his grandfather's life.

We took our cups of tea and biscuits on to the patio in order to obtain some fresh air, enjoy the sunshine and talk about the situation away from the sickroom for a few moments.

Sharon appeared. The beautiful, positive, colourful and life-affirming Sharon was here to support us.

On our return to Terry it was clear that he was fading away from us. Fiona and Sarah were on one side of Terry's bed and Sharon and I were on the opposite side, with Josh holding on to his grandfather's foot with huge tears rolling down and dripping from his chin.

No one could love a grandchild more than I did at that moment. He was sharing the anguish with stoicism and Fiona was her own magnificent self. Whatever would we have done without her? She talked us through what was happening to Terry and her reassurance that there was no pain was a lifeline.

She calmed me sufficiently to allow me to say to Terry, "Thank you for the lovely life you have given me."

And Terry stopped breathing. He was at peace.

Sarah and Josh followed my car home. Josh wanted to sit in my car, but Sarah insisted he travel in hers. This, I suspect, was because she didn't trust my driving in my distressed state; but we got to my village safely and ordered some food from the takeaway, and Josh, darling boy, vacuumed my house through – absolutely everywhere – and then polished my brass sink as if his life depended on it. He wanted to put the world right again. I so loved him.

I had lost my wonderful husband. His decline had been long and heartbreakingly sad, but on that sunny May day, when he had ceased to be with us at all, Fiona and Sharon stayed with us. To say they kept us going is the understatement of all time. They offered nourishment to our spirits and lifted us to another level of awareness as Terry's life drifted painlessly away.

We have lost Terry from our everyday lives. We can no longer visit and hold hands with the man we could physically recognise, but we can be peaceful in the knowledge that our loved one ended his life with gentle hands touching him and with ears which could hear kind and reassuring voices.

Long live Cholwell House, and long live Fiona and all who work with her and listen to her wisdom.

CHAPTER 56

STILL THE WASP STINGS COME, BUT RAINBOWS REAPPEAR

The care never ceased even though my Terry was no more. The feeling of being cushioned from the hurt bombarding my spirit still continued from the carers and nurses at Cholwell.

There was so much to do, so many official forms to fill in: insurances, teacher's and state pensions, funeral choices . . . I was thoroughly daunted by officialdom, and all requiring death certificates and birth certificates. However do people manage?

Obtaining the death certificate at the Guildhall in Bath was fraught for me. Perhaps I am extra-sensitive, but it bowled me over. I had been told to take in Terry's driving licence and passport. To my horror, a large pair of scissors was brought out and the registrar clipped the corners of both these identification documents. It was a bad memory for me and a heartbreaking act to watch.

But things got done and the funeral was on 30 May 2014.

Was this a wasp sting or a rainbow? I still haven't quite worked it out, but Sarah had said to me, "Mum, I want to be a pall-bearer for my dad."

My numbed brain could hardly register her need, and I said, "Sarah, your three big stepbrothers will carry your dad's coffin into church. You are too little." Sarah is very slim and quite delicate-looking.

"No," she said. "My dad carried me, so I want to carry him on his last journey. I will make up the fourth pall-bearer with my brothers."

Who could say no? She was her father's precious child, and Sarah and her firstborn son, Jacob, were the apples of Terry's eye.

To see Andrew, Ian, Jonathan and Sarah carrying their father's body through the church was profoundly moving for all of us. There was great dignity and respect displayed as they travelled through the crowded church.

All was well.

It was to be a burial at Corston Village Church, so everything was in the village which Terry so loved. Service in the church, reception in the village hall and Terry buried in the village churchyard under a beautiful tree full of singing birds.

We played Terry's favourite music and thirteen-year-old Josh wrote and read his own tribute to his grandfather. He said, "My granddad could do anything." Everyone was impressed with his words and by his bravery.

Terry's old friend Bill Horton gave his own tribute. Bill had been chief education officer for Avon when Terry was head of his school in Bath.

Dear Fiona wrote kind, thoughtful words for Sharon to read during the service, and now we had to try and get on with our lives as well as we could.

On the day that Terry died, my brother needed to drive his wife and sister-in-law home to Yorkshire. He then became dangerously ill and was so poorly he couldn't return to be with me for Terry's funeral.

Without him I felt truly alone, but two of my nephews, Darren and Dean, arrived from London to support me and pay their respects to their Uncle Terry. That was a great comfort.

CHAPTER 57

THE DESTRUCTIVE FORCE OF HALF-REMEMBERED WASP STINGS

When the funeral was over and everyone had gone home and attention was directed elsewhere, I found myself in a forlorn and empty place.

Just before Christmas, when Terry was so clearly weakening in body as well as mind, I had decided to retire from my job for the third and final time. I would end my long teaching career when the long summer vacation started in July 2014. This would enable me to devote my entire time and energy to caring for Terry – I would be able to spend every day with him. I had quite often experienced feelings of guilt because I was having a particularly happy and fulfilling day in school whilst Terry was spending his time in his chair without his family around him.

But here I was without a husband to visit and my fulfilling job was coming to an end. I would be absolutely and officially without my work, which had been my passion for so long, in a little more than a month.

Here I was in this dark, hopeless, forbidding and scary place and I had no idea how I was to cope or how I might discover a way of living a rich life in whatever time I had left. I could no longer stride off into the fields or countryside – something I had only dreamed about whilst caring for Terry at home – because arthritis was causing me great pain, particularly in my knees. My despair and sadness overwhelmed me and were fast turning into anger.

I now found myself making long lists in my head of occasions when Terry had caused me frustration and heartache through his need for head-numbing, brain-stopping amounts of alcohol. So many times we had been to functions or school events, especially ones where I might be receiving some acclaim, and he would be frequently glancing at his watch to ensure he had time to get to the pub before closing time. I knew Terry had many demons in his head which could only be swept away with strong drink, but the memory of those disappointing evenings was taking me over, managing to turn pride in my man into all-consuming bitterness.

One day I sat down with pen and paper ready to list the times I had to leave something I was enjoying and go to the pub with Terry or stay and get a taxi home, which I never did. I also recollected that Terry never checked on the time if he was already actually in the pub. I would make a list of those baffling episodes. Those memories of anguish and turmoil, along with leaving behind those moments of purpose and fulfilment which I experienced in school, were causing me to be miserable and apprehensive.

Then from absolutely nowhere came the realisation that making a list of nasty times with Terry would be a gross and monumental betrayal of my wonderful husband. I cannot mark the moment this change of purpose occurred, but the change of direction happened and I felt nothing but relief and enormous satisfaction – as if I had been released from imprisonment. I was whole again and feeling much better. Had I been steered away from something horrible and was God smiling once more?

I had, in the transformation of my thinking, remembered that Terry had told me that his first wife had written a list in an effort to prove his own unworthiness to call himself a husband or a father to their five children. Terry had recounted this story when we first became acquainted, and as he recalled the horror of it he wept. Whatever had possessed me to think of making a list which would prove contempt for a brilliant man who had rescued me from a disastrous marriage, given me a beautiful and free-spirited daughter, given the world inspiring music and also single-handedly created a home I was proud of. With his own hands he had tiled, wallpapered, replaced windows, made a kitchen from a coalhouse, lined walls with timber, fixed electrics and plumbing and built a stone fireplace as well as gardening for us and other villagers, all with such energy, goodwill and stamina that observers were awestruck by his skills and knowledge. Terry had been my lover and my friend and ally. Betraying him was unthinkable.

Terry's composure in the face of adversity was impressive. Once, on the way back from Heathrow Airport in the early hours of the morning, he turned at a roundabout and drove back to the airport because my friend had left a case on the carousel. Utter and complete composure from Terry, but sadly not from me. I just kept repeating, "Whatever were you thinking, you silly bitch?" to my friend Mary, who had accompanied me on a teaching conference in Tunisia. Her companionship had been invaluable and impressive, especially as my expenses had been paid for by London University whilst she had paid her own.

Another time, Terry's composure was tested and sorely stretched when we were in a fast lane on the M62 travelling north. All the electrics went – everything – the lights, the power, indicators . . . We just had the momentum to drift across the traffic and on to a slip road. We had to be towed to a garage, with Terry showing complete self-control. Whilst I was sobbing hysterically at the side of the road, Terry never, not for a single second, lost his cool demeanour.

I am proud that Terry wanted me to be his wife. We had many more good times than bad. We shared incredible holidays together in Sorrento, Madeira, Brittany and Cornwall. We had cruises on the Rhine and Rhône, toured Avignon and visited the chateaus in Normandy eight or nine times. He was my hero and I will love him until the stars fade from the sky.

Now I was in a better place. I would write this book and try to create a club in my village using skills I had developed from over half a century of rescuing children and endeavouring to dispel anxiety and replace life-limiting stress with hope and joy.

That was my decision, and I would be myself again. I was back to my positive and often naughty self.

CHAPTER 58

CONCLUDING THOUGHTS OF
RAINBOWS AND WASPS

Throughout the torments and joyful celebrations of my life there has always been an unbroken thread, which began as a gentle drive and ended as an essential factor in the way I lived my life. My dad always said to me, "If you spoil someone's day by a thoughtless remark you are probably better off dead." This concept ran side by side with my mum's negative attitude to life. A million things could be right in our family life, but my mum would find something that she didn't agree with and out would come angry and dismissive, often poisonous, words which left us all unable to counter them with comforting argument. We were all left feeling uncomfortable, wanting to make everything right but unable to do so. It could be something as simple as a neighbour having a milk bottle on the dining table or a wet sugar spoon put back in the sugar bowl or the finding of a crumb of toast in the marmalade. We could not appease her. She would always find something amiss. Having said that, she was incredibly able to face up to huge challenges. She took on an extra French visitor at Christmas time, so there were six people staying in our tiny council house over the festive period.

A French boy, Guy Maes, had been let down

by his English penfriend, who had refused him accommodation even though Guy had arrived in Bradford for a two-week stay by previous arrangement. My mum was the only person offering Guy somewhere to stay. Her teas were legendary, as were her cleanliness and care of the home. She was fastidious in the detail of her housekeeping, but sometimes that would become a slap in the face.

When I was about ten years old, and sensible enough to boil the kettle, I would get up early to prepare a tray – tray cloth, pot of tea, cups and saucers, sugar and milk, toast, butter and marmalade. I would creep quietly up the stairs, proudly carrying my surprise breakfast for my parents.

Invariably, I would reach the fourth or fifth step and the screeching voice would reach me: "Have you washed your hands?"

The surprise was spoilt and I felt wounded. I would try to keep smiling as I knocked on their bedroom door and as my hands were inspected. I never got used to those spoilt moments. I remember aching for some demonstration of warmth and affection. My dad was too shy and my mum too controlling.

I vowed, from that young age, that if I found a million things wrong I would find one thing that was right and praise it to the sky. I would never knowingly cause someone the hurt which I had felt; and this became my philosophy of life in everything I did, whether it be in school or simply life in general. I try to understand everything and forgive everything. I would try to create rainbows wherever I went. Unconsciously at first and then consciously. Thoughtlessness or simple inexperience I could forgive readily, but if I detected even a hint of intention to harm another person I was relentless in my pursuit of fair play and justice, and I was told many times that my criticism was enjoyed by no one.

I am seventy-six years old now and I feel I've had the richest of lives. Even the soul-wrenching troubles have given me opportunities to not only understand myself, but to reach out to others who have been handed spirit-destroying hurdles in their lives.

Living on this wondrous, intriguing and jaw-droppingly beautiful planet of ours is a privilege beyond measure. Just to watch a sunrise or sunset or see a peacock fan its tail or experience the unique sight of a daffodil dropping its bud ready to open is enough for delight to enter one's spirit and awe to reach the soul. I once actually heard a daffodil dropping its head. Utterly wonderful, like being let into nature's secret world.

CHAPTER 59

MANY TINY WASP STINGS CAN CREATE A PLAGUE

During the time Terry remained at Cholwell House I would, from time to time, write messages to Fiona – notes of admiration for the care that Terry and I were receiving.

Here are some of the letters I placed on her desk explaining how I was feeling before she rescued me. There are two pieces I wrote during the time leading up to Terry moving to Cholwell House. I wanted to let Fiona know how she had rescued me from a terrible and painful existence. I imagine there are many carers enduring similar circumstances who have not yet been rescued. I had written:

June 2012

My husband was such a clever and talented man and he had loved me. When we met forty-three years ago I had recognised his unique greatness. Surprisingly he had chosen me above all his other female admirers especially as I was a rather plump Yorkshire girl who was wacky and had two small children to care for; but we had many happy years together before dementia struck.

I wrote to Fiona, again in June 2012, this small epistle before Terry went away to Cholwell House:

Life is so hard at the moment. Twenty-four-hour care is killing me. I don't know what to do to get myself a little time to be myself and follow one of my many interests. My husband is demanding in a very undemanding way.

As long as I am near he settles and closes his eyes, but the moment I move away he gets up and tries to find me. If I want to go shopping and I employ a carer he still looks for me. Keeping him clean, dressing or undressing him is time-consuming and he can no longer cooperate. Terry is wobbly and unstable and every moment seems fraught with danger. The stress is enormous and I wonder how long I can go on. When he falls he always hits his head. Seven serious head injuries since Christmas!

Olympics, 2012

It was small things which pushed me to the point of despair. During the Olympics 2012 I was fascinated by Mo Farah's ability to spurt forward in the last moments of his race. I was awaiting his run in his second race. I was entranced, riveted and excited by this great Somali runner, running for Britain. Terry chose the final seconds to demand my attention and ask me where his trousers were. I was so angry, but realising he no longer had the capacity to take on board any notion of an interesting story I had to swallow my disappointment. I only needed a broomstick and I could have set myself up as an angry witch!

The realisation that there is absolutely nothing left of my husband's personality or character struck home. My daughter and granddaughter call every other evening and can see for themselves the difficulties becoming unbearable, but their company helps me. The dreadful thing about dementia is that communication is denied only to be replaced with awesome responsibility.

There were moments when I felt I could manage and then I would be shocked into realising that my husband's brain was not functioning at all. The night he tried to wear my bookmark as a watch strap left me in sobbing pieces.

It was Linda finding me hyperventilating at the door as I held on to Terry to stop him wandering or falling that was the moment everything changed and fate led me to you, Fiona.

Linda, my lovely Linda, my daughter with her kind, kind heart and rich intelligence saved the day. Linda was the catalyst which put a stop to the horror of crying all the time with no rest whatsoever, of trying to resist the urge to slap my husband as his behaviour felt perverse. That's when my daughter fixed a week's respite for Terry and me, and from there you rescued us, dear Fiona. I had made an escape from panic, frustration, anger, sorrow, misery and desperation. I felt I had actually escaped from the heaviest of heavy sledgehammers which had repeatedly and mercilessly landed on my poor head.

The following letter was written to Fiona in January 2013:

There must be many people around who now feel as I did just under a year ago. Someone who is nursing a loved one single-handedly and sees that precious person become a little less each day and further away from their original self. Twenty-four-hour care is a mind-boggling enterprise. It is strength-sapping, pitiful, exhausting and extremely demanding on all your resources.

All I wanted to do was to:
1. *Have a little time to myself to think.*
2. *Read a book and lose myself in it.*
3. *Drink a cup of tea or coffee peacefully.*
4. *Chat to a friend.*
5. *Sleep properly without one eye open.*
6. *Walk in the garden or window-shop.*
7. *Sit on the toilet.*
8. *Wash my hair.*
9. *Pluck an offending hair from my chin.*
10. *Choose my clothes for the day without saying, "That will do."*
11. *Be a little irresponsible.*
12. *Watch a play or a film in its entirety.*
13. *Gaze around.*
14. *Listen to the rain on the conservatory roof and feel safe and comfortable.*
15. *Not feel anxiety and constant apprehension.*
16. *Clean my home properly.*
17. *Go to a restaurant and have a 'civilised' meal.*
18. *Find someone who will give me a little while away from my husband so I don't worry at all.*

Dear Fiona, now I have these opportunities, but the guilt sits heavily upon me still – and do you know what your home has done for two messed-up lives? I love my husband – he is my hero. Thank you for the care you and your staff give to him so generously. He does not appear to be suffering in any way at all.

Written to Fiona on 17 October 2012:

Sometimes I feel such a delicious feeling of freedom, and then doom descends on my person and I realise what I have lost from my life forever. Even when I feel like howling like a banshee I know I have to lift myself up and learn to be positive again. I must concentrate on the good things and accept them as real advantages.

- *Terry is mostly physically well.*
- *He sometimes seems to recognise me.*
- *He appears to enjoy the affection shown to him.*
- *He isn't as agitated.*
- *His cough is less worrying.*

I have to accept Terry is now an innocent. He is at our mercy and we are doing our very best to make him comfortable.

Written to Fiona on 6 August 2012 regarding my coping strategies:

Rules I made for myself as I grew in awareness of the devastating effect of dementia.

- *Do not keep reminding the sufferer of the mistakes he has made.*
- *Praise wholeheartedly his few remaining memories.*
- *Keep your voice and demeanour positive and reassuring even when your heart is breaking.*
- *Remember you can only control yourself and your own reactions.*
- *Laugh together even when the source of humour is obvious and slapstick and not in any way sophisticated.*

- *When asked for the hundredth time the same question, just quietly and simply give the answer and do not remind the sufferer that you have answered the same question many times before.*
- *Remember that any exasperation is hurtful to the sufferer and easily transmitted.*
- *Try to persuade yourself that the smell of urine and faeces is good because it means his body is working well.*

Remember to bring your own sense of self-preservation into play if something appears worrying or dangerous. For example, Terry stood on an old drystone wall with electric hedge cutters in his hand in order to begin trimming our hedge – my Hitler routine then came into play in order to get him down safely. The sufferer needs to accept you are not an angel or a saint and that he hasn't total control over all your time and energy. (This was particularly difficult for me because of the constant falling.)

- *Remember that the lost control of the sufferer can lead to displays of anger.*
- *Be loving and caring and vigilant, but try not to become a self-sacrificing wimp.*
- *We are not all-appeasing, compliant, uncomplaining doormats.*
- *Remember, above all, that to live with a vestige of dignity one must not surrender oneself completely to another human being's demands.*
- *Do not press your self-destruct button. Nothing lasts forever, not even the bad times.*
- *Above all else, confide in someone so they know life is not easy and you are hurting.*

Dear Fiona,

I realise from the doctor's words that the blood-thinning medication is no longer halting the TIAs [mini-strokes] and that the strength of the medication cannot be increased. Terry still laughs his old laugh when I joke with the carers and nurses. He still squeezes my hand firmly and looks hard into my eyes. There is something left of my darling husband which reminds me of the life we shared together.

When Terry is hoisted to the toilet I am impressed by the strength which remains in his once powerful arms and I clap and cheer him on. So I want to go on seeing him sitting in his chair at the entrance to the conservatory lounge. I definitely do not want my husband to end his days in hospital.

I more and more want our favourite carer, a Filipino man called Dan, to care for Terry. I so want to shower him and his lovely wife, Mary, with gifts. Mary is so very special and a natural psychologist. One sad day she spotted me walking out of Cholwell House trying to conceal my tears. By the time I reached my car she had wheeled Terry outside to the car park, picked a flower and put it in Terry's hand to give to me as I drove off. Beautiful. A small gesture but a life-saving one for me. We must never underestimate the power of thoughtful care. The simplest action can be a life-changer. Dan will even leave his dinner to go cold whilst he takes Terry to the toilet. This is a complicated procedure involving hoists and wheelchairs and a great deal of patience. God bless positive people and there are so many at Cholwell House.

Thank you, Fiona.
Love from Julie.

30th July 2013
Corston Village

Dear Fiona,

Perhaps you are utterly fed up with reading more of my efforts to be a good wife to Terry. I write in the hope that one day getting my thoughts on paper will help other carers in a similar position, and it helps me to organise my thinking into some coherent message.

I have exactly three days before I go on holiday with our youngest daughter, her husband and their four boys, to Guernsey.

I am terrified. My head tells me to go and have the first real holiday for over seven years, but my heart tells me that I should stay and give what comfort I can to my husband by just holding his hand.

The heartache is compounded by the fact that all Terry's children by his first marriage are also away on holiday, so there will be no family around to nurture what remains of his consciousness.

The care he receives from your staff is magnificent, so I know he will be safe, but I know he is one amongst so many, many residents all requiring your specialist care. When I am there I am there for him. I can feed him, offer him drinks, sing for him, dance for him, wipe his nose and pat his back when he coughs. I can massage his poor thin legs – legs he can no longer use – and hold one of his hands whilst my other hand strokes his neck and shoulders. I know he enjoys this attention because he leans his head into my hand and when I stop he questions me with a look – so I continue. He does not respond to any questions, but there seems to be a kind of communication which allows me to feel valued and needed. Now I feel disloyal and treacherous by leaving him for a *whole week, especially as his life seems to hang in the balance.*

I am told by the visiting doctor that because the TIAs, or mini-strokes, are happening with alarming frequency he may not come round from one of these episodes.

I so need a holiday. I will ring every day from Guernsey, but am I going away, too far away, from my darling innocent man?

I have to give myself a good talking to. Perhaps my wacky and defiant nature will help me through the week away. I must remind myself of the disasters which were the last six or seven holidays. Last year's holiday in Devon was the very worst disaster with the fire in the Scottish castle coming a close second.

I pray for some peace of mind this summer and I pray also that my darling husband will be safe and well on my return.

I hold you in the highest regard, dear Fiona. Such goodness and understanding in one human being is a joy to encounter – and your delicious and wicked sense of humour is a real bonus.

Everyone stay safe and well.

    Julie.

11th August 2013

Dear Fiona,

Can you stand any more additions to the Julie and Terry saga?

It was good to meet your scrumptious husband today. I wonder if he knows how lucky he is to find you and to share his life with you.

    Julie.

CHAPTER 60

THE RETURN

I returned from my holiday – one week on Guernsey with my youngest daughter, her husband and their four boys aged from four (going on forty-five) to fourteen.

Guernsey had been the favourite holiday destination for Terry and me, so I knew I would be faced with painful nostalgia. The boys kept us so busy with our placating techniques that my emotions were held at bay for much of the time. They took it in turns to be stroppy and complained bitterly about some aspects of our provision for their health and safety and amusement, but sometimes they all 'stropped' together.

The oldest one became so disenchanted and disappointed with our efforts to please him that he hid in the wardrobe – twice.

My eldest daughter's daughter, Holly, made up our holiday group to eight. Holly was my lifeline to sanity – but I love them all. Sadly the boys have inherited Terry's bolshie attitude to life and not a lot of my 'niceness'!

Remarkably, leaving Guernsey was much harder for me than arriving there. It was like saying goodbye to Terry all over again. I was swamped by emotion. I was ambushed by my innermost thoughts and memories. Never again will I share the sight of St Peter Port appearing on the horizon, the tiers of multicoloured buildings rising up out of a sea of sailing boats and the masts of yachts, with my remarkable and loving husband. My heart aches and aches, but the worst aspect of my return home was unpacking in an empty house which smelt funny because I'd left a wet dishcloth in the kitchen sink – in all that hot weather!

My son-in-law took my case upstairs. A kind neighbour had cut the lawns, but the wisteria had grown over the security light, and that added somehow to my loneliness when I was left on my own.

I thought, 'What the hell am I going to do with the rest of my life?'

This letter was written in September 2013 from Corstor Village:

Definitely my last letter to you, Fiona. I will not torment you with more of my ramblings. This is just a huge thank you to you and your staff.

My reception at Cholwell House on my return from Guernsey was wonderful. I was welcomed back with such warmth. I held Terry's hand and said to him, "I am your wife and have been for forty-three years. I am your friend and always will be until the stars fade away."

Terry looked at me, searching my eyes for meaning, and gave me a smile. I thank you, Fiona, for keeping my man safe.

CHAPTER 61

ALL THE RAINBOWS TOGETHER

I can't help but believe in guardian angels. We should always allow messages of love and encouragement to sustain us.

These are three of the wonderful letters sent to me which I read when I am feeling low in spirit. One from Linda, my daughter; one from Holly, my granddaughter; and one from Josh, my grandson.

These messages of love keep me going more than anyone would believe:

From Linda:

Early on. . . .
. . . I remember walking along a dusty dirt track
behind the houses in Barrow-in-Furness.
Through a hole in the red brick wall that wasn't
meant to be there
all I could see was barren, weed-ridden land.
My mother sang a loud and happy song
at the top of our voices, kicking our feet, smiling.
We pushed away the bad things
Or we gilded them with twinkle
we strengthened our spirit.
That's what she does, my mother.
She's always done that

That's what she's given us.
Her first instinct is to make the ordinary,
the drab, the dismal
Magical.
I love her most for that.

Happy, happy birthday, precious lady.
Yours,
Linda X

From Holly:

To my beautiful Nanou,
This is just a note to tell you how wonderful I think you are. Thank you for being my Nanou and making me smile and being able to see all the secret wonderful things in the world. And thank you for all of the things you give me, including my beautiful teeth. Even though I do not see you every day like I used to, you are still my bestest friend in the world.
I love you.
From Holly XXXXXX

You really are a special angel.

From Josh:

What Makes Our Grandma Special

She can cook delicious meals and looks twenty years younger than she is.
She can walk with a bad knee and never complain.

*She is so strong she can convince people to drive down tight spaces
with a quarter of a mm to spare between the van and the wall.
She remembers all the good times with our granddad and can even make people happy when they're sad.
We are lucky to have a grandma as nice as you.
You are the best person in the world.
She can make awesome friends that have swimming pools, horses and nice cars.
She is generous with everything she has.
She sees the best in things even when things don't go to plan.
We love our grandma and she loves us too.*

From Josh XXX

CHAPTER 62

RAINBOWS AND PLENTY OF THEM

Once a human being can lift himself or herself from the distressing and futile position of repeating "This time yesterday [or last week or last year or even ten years ago], when I had everything and my loved one could talk to me and we could laugh together . . ." then he or she is on the road to recovery from a great sadness.

Rather better to say now I can:

- Read a book.
- Eat what I like.
- Cook when I want.
- Not cook if I don't want.
- Sleep.
- Nap.
- Watch the birds.
- Talk rubbish on the phone.
- Go to meetings.
- Stare.
- Sit.
- Go to the loo – even sit for a while.
- Pull hairs from my chin.
- Wander about.
- Lose myself in my thoughts.
- Plan ahead.
- Pull weeds from my garden.

- Admire a sunrise or sunset.
- Linger.
- Forget the time.
- Remember birthdays.
- Water my plants.
- Worry about my children and grandchildren without anyone telling me I'm silly.
- Watch a wood pigeon pulling a worm out of the ground.
- Paint my doorstep.

And these are the little things which fill my heart to the very edges and more, and leave my spirit free and my soul ennobled:
- A toddler in a pushchair smiles because I have broken the boredom by playing peek-a-boo behind my handbag in a long supermarket queue.
- I spot a snowdrop or a primrose or a bluebell in an unlikely spot.
- The rain washes off the bird sh— on my car when I've been too lazy to get water and a cloth to wash it off before the rain started.
- I can cuddle a child even when they don't want me to.
- A grandchild says they love me.
- A very ill person wants to hold my hand.
- A neighbour brings me a cake or flowers.
- I knit something which actually fits someone.

So many things can make us feel better. Next, I will, immodestly, relate my biggest compliment of all time.

CHAPTER 63

CONCLUDING WORDS: A COMPLIMENT THAT BECAME A RAINBOW

This is the greatest compliment I've ever received and it is stored in my memory bank for all time.

At one of the schools where I worked, the catchment was overwhelmingly children of Afro-Caribbean origin. Amongst those young people was a young girl in Year 8 (then known as second-year secondary) called Sandra. Her nature was pure exuberance, which often landed her in trouble, and she could often be seen standing outside a classroom where she had been sent for noisily disrupting a lesson. In my mind I had named her as a bit of a problem pupil. English was her first language, so she wasn't in any of my teaching groups, but I had noticed her often.

Break-time duty for staff at this particular school was rather dreaded. We would go out into the schoolyard with our coffee and pray there wouldn't be a fight to deal with. There was nowhere to place one's half-drunk coffee as all the window ledges sloped forward and if you put a mug on the floor it was certain to be kicked over.

This particular day there was a scuffle and shouts from the boys' outside toilet block. I hurried over only to find Sandra and a large group of boys pushing and shoving and yelling. I adopted my Hitler routine with a particular harshness aimed at Sandra, who shouldn't have been in the boys' toilet.

I was just about to return to my coffee when I saw a small girl whimpering inside the cubicle.

She said, "Miss, you shouldn't shout at Sandra. She was trying to stop the boys pushing my head down the toilet."

When class started after break, I went to find Sandra in order to apologise for jumping to conclusions too readily.

I went into the lesson and asked if I could speak to Sandra.

"Oh no, not again – she's always in trouble," said the teacher.

A distrustful Sandra came outside the classroom door and I said, "I'm so very sorry, Sandra, for shouting angrily at you. You were being kind to someone needing help. That is a good thing and you are a good girl."

Sandra said, "You're not so bad yourself, Miss."

There began a wonderful teacher/pupil friendship. She would bring me fresh mangoes and I would heap praise on her for her honesty and helpfulness. Her mother even helped with Caribbean evenings of dance, music and food. She made curry goat and rice and patties and fruit cake for 100 people for one of our evenings. But Sandra's mother suffered badly with arthritis and was sometimes bedridden with the pain. Many Afro-Caribbean women suffer from arthritis in the often inclement and damp climate here in the UK.

One day Sandra told me that her mother had been in bed now for two weeks. Would I go and visit her in Easton, where they lived?

I took some flowers and eggs which I had painted

for Easter, and knocked at the door. A woman I didn't know answered the door and, with eyes like saucers, turned and shouted up the stairs, "It's a white woman." She clearly believed me to be from the police or social services or some other agency which was deemed threatening in this area of Bristol.

Sandra's mother, seemingly worried, dragged herself from her bed to the top of the stairs in order to view the visitor.

With a beaming smile she said, "That's not a white woman – it's Sandra's teacher."

Often 'white woman' is used in a rather derogatory way amongst our Afro-Caribbean neighbours, so it was actually hugely complimentary to know I wasn't deemed 'white'!

CHAPTER 64

RAINBOWS ALL THE WAY TO THE EDGES

These are quotes from oriental philosophers which have helped me on my way.

From Mahatma Gandhi
'An eye for an eye ends up making the whole world blind.'

From an unknown source
'Birds of sorrow fly overhead but you do not have to let them nest in your hair.'

From Swami Vivekananda
'Like the silkworms you have built a cocoon around yourself. Who will save you? Burst your own cocoon and come out as the beautiful butterfly, as the free soul.'

Another from Mahatma Gandhi
'Remember that his own religion is the truest to every man even if it stands low in the scales of philosophical comparison.'

From Thich Nhat Hanh
'It is important to learn how to listen with compassion.

Listening with compassion means listening with the will to relieve others of their suffering, without judging.'

My Own Proverb
'Just because you own a safety pin doesn't mean you are safe.' My translation for my own proverb is this: owning great material riches does not safeguard you from life's difficulties, sadness, hazards or trials. Only spiritual riches can save you.

I try so hard to live up to the sayings made by people wiser than me who have offered their words in efforts to mend the world. Mahatma Gandhi said, *'A profound understanding of religions allows the destruction of barriers that separate them.'* I would add *'ways of life'* as well as religions.

THANK YOUS

Thank you to John Boles, Linda's partner, for his interest and his skill in amending my book and for finding obvious flaws.

To Dean Blake for his belief in me, for taking the trouble to read the first draft and for his thoughtful advice.

I am so grateful for the love, friendship and loyalty shown to me throughout my life and particularly during the very trying times whilst dealing with the bewildering and soul-destroying forces caused by dementia.

Thank you also to all my colleagues at Bristol Metropolitan Academy who believed my contribution was of value.

I am truly in your debt. I doubt I would have survived without your help. Thank you.

FINAL, FINAL, FINAL WORDS AS A POSTSCRIPT

Growing Beyond One's Strength, 6 November 2014
My dad, had he continued to live, would have been 106 today and this notion has left me pondering on the mysteries of life.

My 'no challenge is too much' husband died on 18 May this year, and in so many ways my life is so much easier and less stressful; but also it is more complex and painful.

I want to talk to my dad more than anyone else who has left me behind. I ache to communicate with him and grasp his innate wisdom. He was never too busy to sit and talk, always adding humour to all he offered. I so wish I'd shared more time with him.

Now, what is there to do? I sleep, I nap, I read, I eat, I try to fix the broken bits around my home, I try to help my family, but now this assistance consists of mainly financial support because my legs ache with the relentless effect of arthritis in my joints so moving freely is often difficult. I shop, I drink milky sweet coffee and I smoke cigarettes, but what I most like doing is sitting in my 'thinking chair' and gazing at my magnolia tree, which looks back at me, reminding me of its beginnings, when Terry and I planted it as a twig forty years ago. Now it stands defiantly at more than thirty feet high and forty feet wide.

I have many hopes and dreams still:

- Perhaps this book will help other carers who are coping with a dementia sufferer.
- Perhaps it will help other teachers endeavouring to help young people who are struggling to master English.
- Perhaps it will help anyone struggling to find a safe haven and an escape from heartache.
- Perhaps I am sitting in the eye of a storm with magical rainbows appearing on the horizon.

Yesterday's Rainbow, 28 November 2014

I completed my second day back in school. I was needed because three troubled teenagers had arrived in school – two from Syria (Arabic speakers) and one from Afghanistan (Pashtun speaker) – with little understanding of the English language. Staff believed I could help to settle them and sent for me. Children that I had taught previously actually ran to hug me.

Glorious, wonderful, humbling day. Life can be so good – especially good when a teacher put a card in my bag so when I got home I was able to read, 'Julie Miller, thank you for coming in and making a difference. We love you.'

Our Julie
(Yorkshire Lass)

More than just an English teacher,
No one else could ever reach her.
She engenders skills for living . . .
Faith, empathy and forgiving.
Mighty, modest Julie Miller,
Much more than a classroom teacher.

Partner, mum, friend, daughter, author
And wacky hats made to order.
She is absolutely super
When she swears, like a trooper
Her sense of humour! What a killer!
WE ALL LOVE YOU JULIE MILLER.

Jenny Davis

Rainbows

Creeping to bed on Christmas night
Excitement mounting as we extinguish the light
Jack Frost's finger has etched the window glass
Will Father Christmas stop here?
Don't let him fly past!

Winter diamonds cover the ground
Slippery slides and icicles abound
Children on their way to school, shriek and laugh and tumble
Then winter subsides as spring ushers in
Lightning splits the sky and thunder rumbles.

Going to birthdays in my best party frock
Time only measured with a dandelion clock
Fairies in the garden, rainbows in the sky
A childhood filled with wonder
And so many questions: what and how and why?

Sitting in a lab, learning about day and night
And how to use a prism to split white light
Creating my own rainbow to dance across the walls
The excitement of understanding
And the joy of science now enthrals.

Then one day a rainbow waltzed into my life
A spectrum of colour, an absolute delight!
Blonde hair with red streaks and bright blue eyes
A woman on a mission
Her energy, her passion, took me by surprise.

So our Julie had landed with her own unique gifts
And she loved all our children and teachers to bits
To turn a cupboard to a haven Julie had the knack
She taught and cared and nurtured
She gave everyone a rainbow, everyone loved her back.

Full of affirmation, a smile for every child
They listened to her lessons, totally beguiled
Conflict, loss and sorrow, she soothed away their fears
She taught them skills to face the world
And with a joyful rainbow she replaced all their tears.

To see a soul hurting, always caused her pain
Though into every life must fall a little rain
And when her own dear spirit sank so very low
She wrapped Terry in her love
And turned her sorrow into a rainbow.

I love this Julie Miller, I'm proud to call her chum
With her wicked sense of humour, one can't remain glum
She's a wonderful individual, full of 'get up and go'
And she's given me a special gift
A precious jewelled rainbow.

Eileen Flynn, 3 January 2018

From Abdisalan Mohamed
Sunday 24 December 2017

Dear Lovely Miller,
  Merry Christmas, happy new year, happy birthday.
  I wish we go back to then, when I would come to your little room and be so excited to learn English and hear a new story then get a chocolate bar at the end and treats. THAT WAS THE BEST.
  Enjoy the holidays
  Your sincerely
    Abdisalan